ADAM, EVE, & THE RIDERS
OF THE APOCALYPSE

Adam, Eve, & the Riders of the Apocalypse

39 Contemporary Poets on the Characters of the Bible

EDITED BY
D. S. MARTIN

CASCADE *Books* • Eugene, Oregon

ADAM, EVE, AND THE RIDERS OF THE APOCALYPSE
39 Contemporary Poets on the Characters of the Bible

Poeima Potery Series

Copyright © 2017 Wipf and Stock Publishers. All rights reserved. Except for brief quotations in critical publications or reviews, no part of this book may be reproduced in any manner without prior written permission from the publisher. Write: Permissions, Wipf and Stock Publishers, 199 W. 8th Ave., Suite 3, Eugene, OR 97401.

Cascade Books
An Imprint of Wipf and Stock Publishers
199 W. 8th Ave., Suite 3
Eugene, OR 97401

www.wipfandstock.com

PAPERBACK ISBN: 978-1-5326-3887-9
HARDCOVER ISBN: 978-1-5326-3888-6
EBOOK ISBN: 978-1-5326-3889-3

Cataloguing-in-Publication data:

Names: Martin, D. S. (editor)

Title: Adam, Eve, and the riders of the apocalypse / edited by D. S. Martin.

Description: Eugene, OR: Cascade Books, 2017 | Poiema Poetry Series

Identifiers: ISBN 978-1-5326-3887-9 (paperback) | ISBN 978-1-5326-3888-6 (hardcover) | ISBN 978-1-5326-3889-3 (ebook)

Subjects: LCSH: Poetry—Collections. | Bible—Biography—Poetry. | subject | subject Classification: PS3564.E9268 A3 2017 (print) | PS3564.E9268 (ebook)

Manufactured in the U.S.A.   DECEMBER 26, 2017

For Gloria,
for the glory of God,
& for those captivated by His Word.

Contents

Saints & Stumblers (a preface)	
Words Take Water's Way	Rod Jellema
One Of Twelve	Luci Shaw
Then	Luci Shaw
The Apple and the Knife	Marjorie Stelmach
Cain	James E. Cherry
Enoch	Julie L. Moore
Deluge	Luci Shaw
Prophesy of Birds	Marjorie Maddox
Rainbow For a Fallen World	R. William Muir
Waiting It Out	Luci Shaw
She Was First To Speak	Diane Glancy
Comet-Man's Wife	Diane Glancy
Job Addresses God	Annabelle Moseley
God Answers Job	Annabelle Moseley
Babel	James E. Cherry
Hagar's Lament	Philip C. Kolin
God's Promise	Ona Gritz
Lot	Matt Malyon
Lot's Wife	James E. Cherry
Lot's Daughters	Marjorie Maddox
Abraham's Hand	Ona Gritz
Nothing For It	D.S. Martin
The Sacrifice	Annabelle Moseley
Isaac	James E. Cherry
Rebecca, Pregnant	Ona Gritz

Esau's Lament	Marjorie Maddox
Rebekah Speaks of Jacob	Annabelle Moseley
A Stone for a Pillow	Paul J. Willis
Rachel Looking On	Ona Gritz
Jacob Wrestles With God	Marjorie Maddox
Angel in a Headlock	James E. Cherry
Faith	Angeline Schellenberg
Joseph Dreams	William Foy Coker
Shiphrah and Puah: Midwives in Egypt	Kathryn Locey
Miriam Witnesses Moses' Adoption	Annabelle Moseley
Moses Reclothed	Luci Shaw
Plague	Lynn Domina
One Israelite Midway Across	Lynn Domina
Baal	Christina Lee
In The Basket	Marjorie Maddox
Jephthah	D.S. Martin
Prayer	Jean Bouwman Schreur
King David	Christina Lee
Outburst: The Widow of Zarephath	John Terpstra
Holy Fire	Judith Deem Dupree
A Room In Schunmen	Jean Bouwman Schreur
Poison	Laurie Klein
Elisha's Bones	Julie L. Moore
Amos Speaks at the Richmond Street Exit	Ben Volman
Jonah's Whale Addresses the Almighty	Laurie Klein
Before the Wind	Laurie Klein
Jonah Begins to Think Like a Prophet	Todd Davis
Reluctant Prophet	Luci Shaw
Rib Cage	Luci Shaw
Rage	Lynn Domina
Dry Bones	Lynn Domina
Daniel to the Chief of the Eunichs	Paul J. Willis
The Fourth Man	Marjorie Maddox
Ezra 4	Debbie Sawczak
Choir Practice	Nellie deVries
Song of Joseph: Learning to Read	Barbara Colebrook Peace
Announcement	Luci Shaw
Mary Considers Her Situation	Luci Shaw

Wonder	Julie L. Moore
God Tries On Skin	Marjorie Maddox
Dumbstruck	Christine H. Boldt
Visitation Quartet	Annabelle Moseley
The Nativity	Annabelle Moseley
Visiting the House of Bread	John B. Lee
Unfinished	Nellie deVries
Epiphany	Laurie Klein
Mary Remembers Finding Jesus in the Temple	Annabelle Moseley
The Forerunner	Sandra Duguid
Jordan River	Luci Shaw
Mysterious Ways	Paul J. Willis
Nicodemus's Complaint	Todd Davis
Confession	Julie L. Moore
Mercy	Christina Lee
Lines	Julie L. Moore
The Man Born Blind Sent To See	Lynn Domina
To Live On	Angeline Schellenberg
Memorials	Sandra Duguid
Present	Violet Nesdoly
Martha's Trouble	John Terpstra
How to Go Like Lazarus	Annabelle Moseley
On the Road from Jerusalem	Christina Lovin
A Long Way Off	Laurie Klein
Leaving Paradise	Cameron Alexander Lawrence
Jesus the Christ—Before a Meal	Richard Osler
The Lord Jesus on the Night He Was Betrayed	Debbie Sawczak
Jesus Might Have	Luci Shaw
The Agony in the Garden	Annabelle Moseley
Song of God: for Judas not yet born	Barbara Colebrook Peace
Mary Meets Jesus on the Way of the Cross	Annabelle Moseley
Simon of Cyrene	Mary Lee
Via Dolorosa	John B. Lee
There is No Time for Love to be Born	Christine Valters Paintner
The Disciple Cradles in His Arms the Dead Christ	John Terpstra

Joseph of Arimathea	Marjorie Maddox
The Burial of Jesus	Annabelle Moseley
Magdalen	Philip C. Kolin
James the Less	D.S. Martin
Inviting a Friend to Supper	Paul J. Willis
Emmaus Road Remembered	Luci Shaw
Emmaus	Debbie Sawczak
St. Peter on the Eternity of Threes	Philip C. Kolin
Thomas Didymus	D.S. Martin
Storing Up Treasure	Angeline Schellenberg
Judas, Peter	Luci Shaw
Almost Apostle	Eric Potter
The Thirteenth Apostle	Paul J. Willis
Pentecost	Margo Swiss
Ananias Explains the Situation…	Violet Nesdoly
Ananias Lays Hands On Saul	Todd Davis
Philippi	D.S. Martin
Dwelling	Nellie deVries
Paul's Thorn	Luci Shaw
What James Didn't Say About the Tongue	Luci Shaw
Wandering Stars	Ryan Apple
An Old Man's First Day on Patmos	William Foy Coker
Signs of the Times	Nathaniel A. Schmidt
The Horsemen	D.S. Martin

About The Poets
Acknowledgements

Saints & Stumblers (a preface)

THE BIBLE IS A book of literature — stories and poetry, the inspired reaching of man toward God, and the astonishing reaching of God toward man. It is the stories of people — fascinating people — saints and stumblers — women, men, and angels — and even of the Father, Son and Holy Spirit.

This is a book of literature — poetry about the people in the stories of the Bible. It arises from the meditations and fascinations of ordinary people, albeit quite gifted people, who ask themselves about the significance of these stories for our lives today. Unlike my previous anthology — *The Turning Aside: The Kingdom Poets Book of Contemporary Christian Poetry* — this collection is not about introducing readers to specific poets, but about sharing poems that address specific material. Some of the poets whose work is included are well-known as poets, while some of the others do much of their writing in other forms.

My hope is that this book carries you back into these important stories, that these poems help you to both wrestle with and to be at peace with their mystery, and that they will contribute to the conversations you have with these stories and with the people who have been given to you.

D.S. Martin—Soli Deo Gloria

WORDS TAKE WATER'S WAY *Rod Jellema*

Wave-wash will sand words down
like stones, to shine what they show.
Stranded consonants, dry chunks,
crave the liquidity of vowels.
Words take water's way.
It's like sleep, the slip
through half light while the stars
scatter and move beyond us.
Softer than the air that wakes us,
sleep is water of no weight at all,
loosing us adrift in swirls
of currents, where charts are useless.

When Adam, drowsy, felt
his uncharted ways into speech,
drifting the flow of vowels,
his heart must have leaped like his tongue
from one surprise to the next,
rocks and boulders like sculpted
talismans jutting out, roiling
the river that Yahweh had left him.
And Adam's mouth, holding
the feel of whirl, of crack,
of round, float, and salt,

formed for itself sonorities
of ripple, edge, horse,
of crunch, and moon,
shaping out of the stream of words
his praise and wonder,
the pictures in his head, sounds
that would speak his loneliness,
a few lines that might stay.
He freed all of us, called
Adam's children, to pocket
in our play words like stones

found on the shores, to arrange them
in settings only dreamed,
as many settings
as there are stars in the sky.

ONE OF TWELVE
Luci Shaw

Had the Creator singled out
one of Adam's other ribs
our first mother might have been
impeccable, turning from
the serpent's kiss, spurning
the seething fruit, walking naked
with the man, wanton with light.
Even you and I might have been
born whole enough to swim,
without drowning, the river of
God's will, a race swift as Tigris,
a gold warm as Euphrates.

Imagine a planet without
walls or gates, evergreen,
every frond glossy with spring.
Envision our bodies preserved
for bliss, not lust, not lying,
not dying. Conceive of peace
a pearl shining at the world's heart.
(Yes. And think how perfection tugs,
still, like heaven, at our every cell.)

Eve, though, was the chosen bone
(in which our own dry skeletons
lay layered, waiting for breath),
one of twelve, like Reuben who went
up to his mother's bed, or Judas,
grabbing his bloody silver,
or December, darkest of a year
of months. Yet January's chill,
the death of gardens, harks back
by a dozen days to the Advent Seed
dug in to die, sprouting its
improbable winter green shoot
for which we wait—a garden not

in Eden but in us—Epiphany,
unflawed fruit of the twelve
days of Christmas.

THEN

Luci Shaw

It was then the nettles descended
and covered their nakedness with burning
golden leaves, and the grasses bowed
their heads and breathed "Trouble, trouble,"
and anguished, the thorny vines unsheathed their
barbs, and the very clay from which he came
regretted its yield, and the rib at her core
went bone-white and groaned
as the Lord God roared at them both
with words of fire that hurt worse
than stings and spikes and grass fires,
and it was clear that a pestilence
had spread through the wild. Even the tree
at the heart of the woodland felt shame
for producing a fruit that provided
an occasion for sin. And it was then that
the reptile hid his smirking face
and slid into the undergrowth, satisfied.

THE APPLE AND THE KNIFE *Marjorie Stelmach*

A recent study shows that "the mere act of peeling an apple will stimulate taste in the central lobe."

A *study*? sneers my love. My taxes paid for *that*?

But I'm picturing the apple and the knife—
one in each hand—
        and considering
dexterity: how the apple-hand, statistically,
turns out to be the sinister one.

He isn't listening anyway; statistically,
                he's thinking of sex.

But I'm thinking of the Garden:
no blade to be had, her mouth turned
        weapon—tongue and teeth and lips
all drenched (no time to think)
in a luscious wash of appetite,
        her left hand fallen—
empty, open—to her side.
What then?

Love might still be thinkable. Even
help-meet. Even *gift*.
        But not for long. As the artists
of *Expulsion* have abundantly shown,
unlike her man, she'll need, poor Eve,
        both hands to hide her shame,
when the blaming ends and
the nakedness begins.

CAIN

James E. Cherry

God has never had to explain anything:
why old faithful breeches every 63 minutes,
a leopard has never lost a spot or why
the fat portion wasn't good enough.

As an ex-patriate of the earth, you discovered
a wife and sanctuary east of Eden, a spot of land
to subdue the flesh, silence the spilling of blood.
All your days were spent building homage

to Enoch with the call of God on your forehead,
the same God you wanted to seize
by the throat before you invited your brother
to go for a walk instead.

ENOCH

Julie L. Moore

First there was the twitch
        of the olive leaf lipping its stem,
                then the sigh of silt, settling,
                      and the surrender of crickets,
                              their legs, like fans, folding,
                      when the trill of a brook,
            intoxicating, irresistible,
    like the grace of his Lord,
carried him away that evening—
        no chariot for Enoch
            at the age of 365
                who walked with God
                  and simply
                            like the last day in a year
                              was no more.

DELUGE

Luci Shaw

Think, if you were left behind.
A dead calm, sinister, then the first drops
and the river beginning to rise until
the tender tips of the grasses vanish, the wind,
the weeping trees, and days later
from the beach the wooden craft lifting,
buoyant with twinned animals. You listen,
as the unlikely prophet and
his raucous offspring shout
goodbye to your doom and outrage.

Then the drenching gloom. Pewter waves
stretching to every horizon with only
a far shadow mountain left of terra firma,
brine climbing your chilled limbs as
your mingled roars and tears meet the sky's.
Maybe you thought good fishing
when it started. Now you're the dead fish,
or will be when you've quit treading water
and water drowns out air and everything
is over. And under.

THE PROPHECY OF BIRDS   *Marjorie Maddox*

The Raven

knew flight over waters when all there was
was wet, the ark lost behind the smooth arch
of wings, only a thin line of air
between green sea and grey sky,
then forever and forever
washed up with the slap
of wave against wave.
What weariness to circle
the same expanse,
the echo of rain,
even the wind
unable to land,
looking,
looking.

The Dove,

pale
shadow
tracing the raven's
soar above an earth-
turned-sea, seeking—
for seven days—any inch
of dry, finding only the man's
chapped hand. The second week,
its flight fingered the tops of waves
that fingered the tops of trees, releasing,
finally, twigs of green ready for the dove's sleek beak.
Its last journey knew no U-turns, just a straight flight
to elsewhere, brimming with bushes, drenched orchards
hungry for song, hallelujahs hanging from every waiting bough.

RAINBOW FOR A FALLEN WORLD   *R. William Muir*

Mourning for a sinful age
The waters crest, the winds enraged
God has boldly set the stage
      for the aftermath

Silence in the dead of night
The clouds obscure the stars from sight
Waves engulf the mountains' height
      in a watery tomb.

White dove in the fresh dawn air
A sign to us of answered prayer
Hope has risen from despair
      With an olive branch

Yahweh's banner, Yahweh's word
The promise of our God unfurled
Rainbow for a fallen world
      In the morning sky

WAITING IT OUT *Luci Shaw*

*"How long will you say these things, and
the words of your mouth be a great wind?"*
—Bildad, to Job

Swung on a string between the will of God
and the clutch of Satan, this is pure wretchedness.
You have made a list of tawdry, self-justifying
statements but your friend endlessly
considers your excuses a mere whine of wind.

He and his allies view you as a specimen
of failure, your body a battlefield of sores and
visible bones, hair matted, eyes wild with looking
to heaven and pleading, pleading to be judged fairly.
You are not yet a cadaver available for
forensic investigation, and this is no idle
philosophical discussion with either God or men.
Rather, a prolonged confrontation

in which the pious hanker to be proven right
and righteous so that they can believe themselves
superior: "See? Unlike you, we are not pawns
of the powers!" And because your body is
too weakened to be energized into coherent response,
you wait for heaven to transmit answers so
you don't have to. You wait for the harsh words
to die down, for some blessed
silence.

SHE WAS FIRST TO SPEAK *Diane Glancy*

Job talks with his friends.
Would they ask me to join them?
I stand silent as a wind turbine on the high plains.
Where are my words that lift the flat sheet of the world
to address the suffering and dilemmas therein?
They leave me out.
To be without words!
The stubbles hurt my feet.
The Universe ate our first children.[1]
We all are expendable.
This Mystery. This Unanswerable.
This Old One up there who spoke the world into being.
But I remain silent?
What skies are these? To whom do they belong?
Tell me where you are. What you see.
What God is there with Satan rolling around his throne
saying, give me Job for a moment?[2]
Are there other worlds? Isn't this one enough?
All those buzzings of comets and falling stars
in the observatory in Uz. Those astro-heads. Those Job's friends.
I would debate the arguments if I had their bag of words.

1 Job 1:18-19
2 Job 1:11, 2:3-4

COMET-MAN'S WIFE *Diane Glancy*

What do I know of the God Job heard? What do I know of the universe? I wait on the tarmac in Uz for my flight. What longing to be elsewhere than this Earth— Why can't we just have Earth? But the terrible stars *thwock* over us with their noise. They are bright and sharp as bee-stings. I swat them. What bee-blaze before us? What sting, this Earth? I watch Job suffer. I have no investment in this. He saw something I did not— We hold these multiple views of the Universe. He talks to God but I see no one there. His convulsions— his conclusions are not for everyone. A stone falls in a straight line for one. The same stone falls in a parabolic curve for another. Why did he hold so steady in his views? My husband taught the children. How did life come to be on Earth?— *God*, they answered. Is there life somewhere else in the Universe?— *The Lord God in his Threesome*. Can we communicate with the Godhead?— *Yes, through prayer*. In this way the Universe is sacred. Who is this God who throws a puzzle to trip us up? It's his way or no way. If only God would share what he knows. He takes my seven sons and three daughters and puts more sons and daughters in their place. Jemimah, Keziah and Keren-happuch are the new girls' names.[3] Did he think all was mended? I hear the cries of my first sons and daughters. The loss of thousands of sheep, donkeys, oxen and camels.[4] Job watches the planets through his telescope, his parchment rolled into a tube. These nights are a field of bees. The spears of stars fall past us. This star watcher, this comet-man. Have you not heard? Job said to me. He walks in the circuit of heaven.[5] I think of space rolled as parchment into a tube through which the planets pass. If only we were alone here— without the Watcher— the bee-keeper— over us. The planets circle the sun on their course, their roll-ways, their little corridors. A children's game. But this is not a game. We are the condensation of elements from this far-off God. We live. We suffer. We are gone. What do I know of peace?

---

3 Job 42:14
4 Job 1:14-19
5 Job 22:14

JOB ADDRESSES GOD　　　　　　　　　　*Annabelle Moseley*

Then Job began to tear his cloak and cut off his hair.　Job 1:20

The silence is all. Though I want to split
the stillness of this day with fractured cries,
and tear this room apart, I will admit
that such a sundering would not be wise.
What would it do to shatter every dish,
or smash the vases, break each cup and bowl?
How would that change what I've begun to wish—
that I could go right back to being whole—
even if it meant forgetting you and
the great pain that loving you has brought? I—
I tore my hair today. You understand?
My clothing, too. I wait for you to cry
out, ask me not to harm myself. I won't.
But I know loneliness. And God, you don't.

GOD ANSWERS JOB *Annabelle Moseley*

Who is this that obscures divine plans with words of ignorance?...
Where were you when I founded the earth? Job 38:2-4

You say I don't know loneliness. What, Job,
you've never seen the chasms between stars?
Observe the distance of your heart, then probe
yourself for answers. Look down at your scars.
You think I put them there, I know. But pain
is from your world, not mine. And all the while
I plan my entrance. Gardens all need rain
to raise their beauty. My plot grows a trial
of such deep suffering, the torn curtain
of a great temple will be how I rend
the earth of sleep. Sacrifice makes certain
a love that will not hesitate or end.
Mend yourself, now. Follow my command.
(I'm pierced in ways you'll never understand.)

BABEL

James E. Cherry

God heard the rumors, word on the street,
the whisper of innuendo, cries for a coup d'etat.
After all, He is the original grapevine.

And the day He visited the work site,
He was impressed with the quality of materials,
the sleek design, the dedication to deadlines

before He made deaf their ears
with the sound of their own voices,
abandoned lives in search of lost tongues.

GOD'S PROMISE   *Ona Gritz*

Genesis 21:1-3

My husband's hand
on my stooped and tired shoulder.
His fingers finding my breasts
in the old way.

I swear, in the dark,
I could be twenty tonight,
meeting that warmth
as though it were chill air.

Sarah, he says,
and there's breath in the name.
My tongue seeks his neck,
soft now, lined.

He cries out just as I feel it.
One forgotten egg
slipping through me,
lit with heat like a star.

HAGAR'S LAMENT

Philip C. Kolin

My son was more destined than
Any of the caravan children
Suckled on the thistle milk
Of course-browed maids
Who found his favor
Only once
And then left
To journey through his adopted land,
Orphaned.

My son was cool sunlight
In his father's sight.
Laughter gamboled with
Time's potency to voice
The capture of age by my womb's desire.

My bonds were love's trinkets
Shackles to hold his eye.
The time was free for us;
We coupled with the law.
My son under Sinai played a tabor
While his father slept.

But not restfully.
Nightly his calls to me
Fretted with the aches
Of a man uncomfortable with his flesh.

His kindness wandered.
He heard Sarah as if God spoke
Violets and jasmine on her lips--
An old garden to plant his treasure.

The other one looked as pale as bread.
And I in my prime took the salty wilderness

As my consort--a covenant of arrows
Flailed my heart; I hide my pride.

But God opened my eyes to wells
Deeper than the Red Sea;
My son's sons all darkened
In the promise that baptized
The offspring she weaned
In the shadows of my tent.

LOT

Matt Malyon

Genesis 19

My gaze so fixed on the holy,
I had all but forgotten

the feel and look of her face.
My daughters, too, beautiful

and innocent, were strangers—
the easier to offer them.

Who can judge? The two angels,
heralds of the rumored doom,

were under my protection.
                                      Weeks
later, returned to my cave, I watched

the cities of the plain stilled
to ashes, unable to tell

where last she'd stood, how long I'd sat
beside the pillar. Even the feel

of my arms around her brave turn
a memory now, the taste of her

hardened lips less salt than fire.

LOT'S WIFE

James E. Cherry

History has deemed you unworthy of a name,
 the mere property of Abraham's nephew,
a case study on the perils of possessing the past.

But maybe, in your haste for the hills, the photos
of you and Lot at the beach flashed
across your mind or maybe a coffee pot

on the fire came to remembrance or the dog barking
to be walked or fed woke you from daydream.
These are the things of speculation. What we know

for sure is that your life has become a moral
to an Old Testament story, a footnote upon the history
of fire and brimstone, indelible as a glance over the shoulder.

LOT'S DAUGHTERS

Marjorie Maddox

Genesis 19

I.
At first—a leering mob circling
the house, jeering, dancing naked,
taunting the guests with their sex—
the daughters thought their father brave
to step outside, lock the door behind him,
stretch his arms out in protection.

But then, even he offered them up,
a sacrifice to protect strangers,
their father, the only
"righteous man" in a city destined for flames,
"Do with them what you like.
But don't do anything to these men."
 Then their eyes were like Isaac's
below the knife,
the ram not yet in the bush,
the blade gleaming.

II.
What dread dug in the daughters'
betrayed hearts before the rioters—
struck blind—stumbled and fell,
unable to find the door,
Lot tugged back safely to the house?

Eyes straight toward Zoar,
did they hear their mother turning,
nostalgia sliced mid-sentence?
That life left behind,
what fixed their gaze away
from home—their father's almost-sacrifice,
or the intervention?

III.
No mention of mourning.
Their mother's unbelief behind them.
Too many miles.
The sun hot as horror.

IV.
When they fled to the cave
with no hope for heirs,
ashen cities behind them,
mercy was an unremembered flame.

This time, they sacrificed themselves,
holding out wine, lifting their dresses
to lure their father.
He twirled a drunken dance,
love or revenge spinning,
blurring vision.

"Rewarded" with sons,
they named them From Father
and Son of My People,
sang lullabies of fear and fire,
of what it means to wander,
to exile yourself,
to dream of salt and sand.

ABRAHAM'S HAND *Ona Gritz*

Genesis 22:1–12

As though they were your own,
you know the sloping lines
and dry patches in your father's palms.
The calluses on his fingertips
like small coins hidden in the skin.
You know the crevice of a scar
between two right knuckles
and the dark pattern of hairs above.
He has given you tools and shaped
your fingers around them
to show you their uses,
mussed your hair and passed you
countless baskets of bread.
As a baby you clutched his rough finger
the way birds wrap their feet
around branches to stand.
Now he comes to you saying,
"Walk with me to the mountain"
and holds out his hand.

NOTHING FOR IT *D.S. Martin*

No point trying to sleep that night
Nothing for it but to rise early
& saddle the donkey   My son after all
was dead   He & I walked
beside the beast   that bore the wood
& the servants   who bore the fire
Something must have betrayed me
for we talked   not at all   till sundown

On the third day I lifted my eyes
to the distant mountain   Here
was where the knife must fall   The rest
was like a dream   I bound my son
who showed complete trust   as I
went through the cold motions of slaughter
but my hand was stayed
& God showed his provision

On the third day   my son who was dead
was raised again

THE SACRIFICE   *Annabelle Moseley*

I. Abraham Addresses God

You knew I would withhold nothing from you.
Why would you ask for me to kill my son?
What if he was your boy? What would you do?
Have you ever known pain? For I've begun
to question why you'd test me that way. He
was young, my only child, asked me where
we'd find the sheep to slay. He trusted me.
I still have dreams at night about my prayer—
to you—as I bound Isaac, as he cried—
I told you he was yours to take. I'd raised
that child—and now raised my knife. Provide
me with a reason. Was I numb? Or crazed?
I know your angel stopped me, God, but why
ask me to kill to prove that I'd comply?

II. God Answers Abraham

It is not disrespect to question me.
I saw the way that Sarah looked at you
when Isaac told her God had set him free.
She wondered if you would have followed through—
and killed her boy. But just as I gave birth
to Isaac with her help, I gave him life
again—through sparing him I taught the earth:
I don't want children carried to the knife.
Your Isaac bore the sacrificial wood
upon his back. But one day, Abraham,
I'll know your pain. On that day I'll make good—
I'll give my sacrifice for you—my lamb;
carry, like wood, the pain that Isaac knew—
give what I wouldn't take away from you.

ISAAC   *James E. Cherry*

Halfway to Moriah, you keep adding up fire, wood
and that strange look in your daddy's eye, keep getting
the same number no matter how many lambs you subtract.

At the mountain, you understand the nature of mathematics
strapped to a burnt offering, the glint of a blade blinding
your eyes and when your turn your head to cry *Abraham*,
a bleating sheep screams your father's name.

REBECCA, PREGNANT

Ona Gritz

Genesis 25:19–25

The tight wet sack my twin boys
share is a battlefield. One aims
a forming foot at his small curled brother.
That one retaliates, using an elbow
sharp as a gnawed chicken bone.
Be grateful for the gift of sons,
says Isaac. And I am.
But, sometimes, half sleeping,
I envision daughters.
They lay quietly, head to head,
touching palms.
Awake, I drink a ladle-full of milk
and it fuels this fight. *What's the point,* I ask,
if they wish to cancel one another out?
Our God is nonchalant. Already,
He's decided which of my two children
I'm to love.

ESAU'S LAMENT
Marjorie Maddox

Without your words   my breath cracks
    dust on sand   without your words
my limbs break   bones on graves
Oh my father   me too   without
    Can even this be stolen?   your words
No syllables of blessing left?
       No mouthed morsel of hope?   Oh my father
I alone am the hunted   your words
    trapped and slain   me too
the spoils stolen again   me too
      that fair enemy
              without without

REBEKAH SPEAKS OF JACOB

Annabelle Moseley

I knew it was not something he'd outgrow.
He was a fighter. Weak, the smaller twin,
my Jacob clutched his brother's heel at birth;
it was innate to strive, vital to win.
A stairway shadowed everything he did.
He lived to climb. The blessing was his due.
But when he ran away, some called him cursed.
Jacob will find a ladder to break through
the clouds until he claws at heaven—finds
a way to get a blessing right from God
Himself. That's how ambition is designed—
to keep on trying till you get the nod.
No parent can resist the child who tries—
and God's a parent. He'll hear Jacob's cries.

A STONE FOR A PILLOW   *Paul J. Willis*

*Taking one of the stones of the place, he put it under his head
and lay down in that place to sleep.* Genesis 28:11

When you had a stone for a pillow,
      stone for a pillow,
           what did you dream?

I dreamed there was a ladder to heaven,
      ladder to heaven,
           star and gleam.

When you saw the ladder to heaven,
      ladder to heaven,
           who climbed there?

The angels of God went up and down,
      up and down,
           step and stair.

After the angels went up and down,
      up and down,
           what did you do?

I set my pillow up for a pillar,
      up for a pillar,
           dawn and dew.

When you left your stone set up for a pillar,
      up for a pillar,
           where did you go?

I went to my uncle's to seek a wife,
      seek a wife,
           long ago.

RACHEL LOOKING ON *Ona Gritz*

Genesis 29:16-30

Here is a dream we've all had,
the one where you watch
yourself from a distance,
as an onlooker or a kind of god.
Today, it's my wedding I can't
wake from. There I am,
hidden in my mother's lace,
holding my father's arm.
My husband-to-be
mouths my name with a love
I have felt like sun on my shoulders
as I've crouched in a garden,
picking greens. Now, he takes
my hands in each of his,
begins repeating vows.
This other me is taller than I,
her hands broader than mine.
But in such dreams no one
notices, and I can't call out
for I'm only eyes.

JACOB WRESTLES WITH GOD *Marjorie Maddox*

Genesis 32:22–32

      What daring, and only a wrenched hip
and changed name to stumble home on.

Israel, we call you now,
      you who pinned God and forced a blessing,

      who pressed Yahweh's face to the ground and lived.
O Deceiver, who stole your brother's birthright.

O Defrauder, who duped a blind father;
      faithful fighter, strong-holding the Strong,

      how mightily the Almighty must love you,
His mercy overpowering

the flimsy might of your muscles,
      the bruised strength of your repentant soul.

ANGEL IN A HEADLOCK   *James E. Cherry*

You were the daughter your mother always desired:
sensitive to solitude, appreciative of the arts, skillful
over a hot stove. You were an equal opportunity trickster
of brother, father, father in law, always looking
for an opportunity to toss a tent to shelter
your insecurities and fear. But this night
on the other side of the Jabbok, the earth is
a squared speck of dirt, has become shadows
of grasp and release, a place of mirrors and mercy
where daybreak limps just above the horizon.

FAITH
Angeline Schellenberg

I am not like Jacob: I
had no twin to wrap my arm
around as we slept. No nightly
angels climb down my darkened
stare or dance under my pin as I
dream on this lonely, God-forsaken rock.

But I too have fought through blackness,
groping for the twisting arm of
a strangeness that won't let go before
it blesses me. I too have grasped
a nearness that ached to slip me
out of joint, wrest from me old names,
old ways of limping.

JOSEPH DREAMS

William Foy Coker

always confined always constrained
from Dothan's cistern to the Midianite ropes
from Potiphar's house to his prison walls

but at least this pillow's softer than
my father's rock at Bethel
and I know Adonai is with me

if only I could dream my way up his stairway
ascend with angels of God out of this place
blow like dust back to the land of promise

don't want to be anyone's idol
don't need sheaves or heavenly bodies
bowing down to me

don't want any earthy Egyptian
women smelling of cistus roses
playing out their lusty dreams on me

yes Adonai keeps granting favor
and most days warden's work keeps me busy
busy enough so there's no daydreaming

but some nights these dragging days
set my teeth on edge like grape clusters
clinging to their branches

two years of stale dry days growing
moldy as baskets of white bread left
forgotten in this forlorn corner

I start to wonder if Adonai sleeps—
does he slumber dreaming me as symbol
for something too vast for me to grasp?

then this dark place and my heart begin
to lighten with reassurance
and the words come comforting

time to lift up your head you dreamer
lift up your head to Adonai
before Pharoah lifts it up for you

SHIPHRAH AND PUAH: MIDWIVES IN EGYPT   *Kathryn Locey*

We refused to kill babies.
Well, not refused exactly—failed—
said we arrived too late to the labors
of those hardy, headstrong Hebrew women,
who popped out infants like they were ripe
fruit—figs, maybe, or apricots—
then hopped up and went right back to making
bricks with no straw, bread with no yeast,
love with no thought
of reaping woe in nine months' time.
"Who knows what happens to the babies?"
we asked, our faces blank as papyrus scrolls.

So that is how Moses, his mother,
the basket-boat, Egypt's daughter, ten plagues,
and the freedom of a people happened.
Because Pharaoh knew nothing about women.

MIRIAM WITNESSES MOSES' ADOPTION *Annabelle Moseley*

The river joined two women's gifts that day.
My baby brother floated in between
the strength to give a treasured son away
and courage of adoption. Crouched, unseen,
my long hair blending with the river reeds.
I bit my hand, afraid I'd intervene,
and shout to Pharaoh's daughter of his needs,
the way laughter could always soothe his cries,
the way he played with mother's wooden beads.
And as I watched, I slowly realized
it was as hard for that princess to choose
to take him; as for us to compromise—
guarding his innocence from evil's sway.
The river joined two women's gifts that day

MOSES RECLOTHED

Luci Shaw

Bare-soled he waits,
bowed bare-headed, stripped to the heart,
eyes narrowing, hands to his face
against the heat,
watching.

Hissing, the dust-dry leaves
and cobwebs shrivel
baring the curved thorns
woven with gold,
and the black-elbowed branches
wrapped in a web of flame.

Wondering, he waits
in the hot shadow of the smoking voice—
observes no quivering flake of ash
blow down-draft from the holy blaze,
no embers glowing on the ground.
Flinching, himself, before the blast
he sees the un-shrinking thorny stems
alive, seared but still strong,
un-charred, piercing the fire.

Enveloped now in burning, ardent speech
he feels the hot sparks touching his
tinder soul, to turn him into flame.

PLAGUE

Lynn Domina

The first one you see
squats suspiciously between your shoes,
his green flesh pulsing with breath, his white belly
faintly damp. Then you see two
hop onto your flour sacks, their quick tongues
lashing out, in. A monstrous
female pauses on your own chair;
her huge nearly reptilian eyes
lock onto yours.
Inside your cupboard, dozens
tumble upon each other, caught,
tangled in their own limbs, and their heaving abundance
roils your empty stomach. Outside, the land

vibrates, membranous with their slick skins,
until you can't bear
setting your foot anywhere, neither on stone nor sand
nor your own precisely tiled terrace. You imagine
the village well clogged
with bleating bullfrogs that never sleep, your still
water foaming with eggs, their young
brushing your lips with each sip. Some foreigner's god
curses you again, you, who never
did more than prepare
your husband's favorite sweet, swaddle his sons,
brush his hair evenings
as he repeated rumors of the stuttering murderer
who plagued Pharaoh's court with commands,
threatening them all with tricks
any magician could outdo.

ONE ISRAELITE MIDWAY ACROSS   *Lynn Domina*

The wall of water rippled,
barely contained by a fine shimmer of something
almost unreal. He paused in panicked flight,
slid his hand gingerly into the diaphanous sea, cupped
his palm beneath a blue fish's belly.
Gills pulsed, alive. He stood
on dry land, the living water risen above him,
trembling with creatures, his hand
stroked by pectoral fins, until the fish swam away and he
ran on.

BAAL   *Christina Lee*

Why not
balk at bitter water
from a struck stone?
Why these meals alone,
watching the sky for bread
like fish snapping
at pond scum?
Why all this rot? Why not
keep all we hoard? Why not
a god to hold, a shape we know?

IN THE BASKET

Marjorie Maddox

Her temptress hands entwine us,
uncoil the rope, lower us over
the city wall, our lives and promise
dangling from her fingertips.

In our clandestine eyes, she sees
her small sisters
safe, her brothers alive, the parents
we will not burn when we return.

The basket jerks; her arms tense.

She wears our oath like a scarf
taming her wild hair
with repentance
and does not speak.

We are almost down.

Rahab—small, dark ship
on the wall's horizon
from which we are floating away—

stretch your scarlet sail tight,
embrace your family.
Before the moon swells,
our God will blow his anger
over the city's crest,

but you, brave one,
he will let go, now safe
in his boat-basket
of grace.

JEPHTHAH   D.S. Martin

In the jingle jangle morning
Jephthah   judge of Israel   came triumphantly home
with clink armour
& clatter carts
his bold vow hardly reconsidered
on the dust-foot   foot-sore march

Well-earned aches sang of victory
bastard days behind
brothers in his debt
his vow a bet against giving his best?   Perhaps
He should never have taken the chance
for first through the front door   plainly seen
the lamb to be slaughtered   his only daughter

Her light-foot celebration dance
& tambourine   with skipping reels of rhyme
in no time   transformed to misery

Leave it to scholars to show Shakespeare
foreshadowing Ophelia's death
Spirit prefiguring Calvary

She walked the hills in a long black veil
a virgin daughter mourning   what would never be
granted two months to roam
The smoke swirl like water whirl
stood   forever   between her   & her wedding day
In the jingle jangle morning
he came stumbling   home

PRAYERS

Jean Bouwman Schreur

1 Samuel 1 & 2

Year after year
I longed to remain home,
silent
and complete.

Year after year
I traveled to Shiloh for worship.
Surrounded by a crowd of men, women, and children,
I, troubled and broken.

Year after year
I choked down the double portion
into my barrenness. A relentless
void.

Year after year
I prayed out of my great anguish and grief. Laments,
cries and pleas. Unwritten
prayers scored on my heart.

Until one year,
my drunken prayer became
the song of flesh and bone.
And became the prayer remembered.

KING DAVID
Christina Lee

coined the phrase
better to beg
forgiveness than
ask permission.
Quick to praise,
slow to listen.
Runt of the litter,
kid-brother. Singersongwriter.
That voice
could slip
the crown
off a king, honey
from the rock. Owner
of an overflowing cup
and backstock
of sackcloth.
Envy of men, kingpin
of plots. Dancing
queen, smooth
talker. Crack shot.
Aiming straight
for God's heart.

OUTBURST: THE WIDOW OF ZAREPHATH   *John Terpstra*

     Every day I go outside and is it
    not nice weather we're having? I tell
      the same joke. Every weather it's
     the same nice I'm going on about

          How dry
        a drought is

                    It's only dust
                          keeps the dancing up
                   and only wind
                          keeps the dust up &

    I ohmeohmyoh clap in time
 our earthy dervish land bland sand

        I want rain
          water
        torrents
         floods

I want thunder and lightning & to see some clouds
 so black they blot the blue blue blue so bad
  you can't concentrate on the fact it's day

                     I want
                     a wisp
              as big as my fist
      to give me a hint of hope right out of the
      blue
                        but no
                    nothing

        not a whisper of anything
         between us and heaven.

                              Disaster surely
            shakes things up, starts you thinking saying
            what would have shocked yourself yesterday
                    like today, praying, either it rains
                              Lord
                         or Lord we die

so who'll break first?

HOLY FIRE
Judith Deem Dupree

*Then the fire of the Lord fell, and consumed the
burnt offering and the wood and the stones and
the dust, and licked up the water...* I Kings 18:38

It all boiled down to this: Elijah at his makeshift
altar, drenching twelve great stones, the wood,
the sacrificial flesh. Bloody water pooling
in the trenches. His lone voice hollering to JHWH.

And then, the sudden terror of His people,
standing by; flames exploding wildly from
the sludge before them, devouring the whole
of it. Boulders shattered feebly down to ash.

The howls of the prophets of Baal gone dry in
their throats. That empty swath of earth,
its oily black scar, the smell of charred fat.
Fear hovering above the hillside like the vapor

wrung from rock—a bitter incense, gritty
exhalation—heavy upon them each, this acrid
Cloud of their Unknowing, And then, its
sudden lifting. The great Unheard: "I AM."

A ROOM IN SHUNEM   *Jean Bouwman Schreur*

2 Kings 4

I watch a fox wander the field,
through straight green rows
into the woods to find her den.
A bird disappears into the tree branches and finds her nest.
In the distance, I see the holy man of God.
Tonight he will rest in the room prepared for him,
a room with a bed and table, a chair and lamp.

I offer a place of quietness and peace.
He, in turn, promises a foolish dream.

He sees me coming in the distance,
running in distress, anger and bitterness,
with surrender and panting faith.
The foolish dream has broken my heart.
I tell him the room is quiet and peaceful,
the bed, table, chair and lamp.
A room full of no breath, waiting for resurrection.

POISON

Laurie Klein

2 Kings 9:33–37

Don't blame the dog, exponentially
sick, as if five Great Danes gorged
on roadkill, then field grass, then
relieved their ills in your home. Sad dog
never meant to ruin your Persian rug,
fit for a palace. And look, he's still
not eating. Neither are you,
three rolls of paper towels gone,
half a bottle of Pine Sol.
All week, all the windows
                            stay open.
Can you see two ancient eunuchs
bent over a balcony, gagging
as horses trample the fallen queen?
Then the dogs, their feral take-down,
rolled in. Consumed. The horror,
and pity, the unpardonable relief
at all that curdled Jezebel's soul,
the ungoverned lust, and conceit,
the primeval lightning-rod need,
calling down claw and tooth and jaw,
the cleanup crew sickened, for days.

ELISHA'S BONES   *Julie L. Moore*

2 Kings 13:20-21

What was it like
in such a burial,
tossed into another's tomb,
ears deaf to the men's
shouts beyond you,
feet numb to the pebbles
pressing upon them,
breath escaped like a prodigal son,
and eyes blind to the prophet
dead beside you?

Sudden and insane,
you collided with his frame,
lingering power of God
seeping from his side
infusing your soul,
and once again,
you heard your heartbeat
suffocating silence, you found breath,
coughing dust from your chest, your toes
dug into the ground below them,
you saw light.

And you knew your place,
as though you were Adam
emerging again from clay,
the bones of Elisha having released you
from your grave.

AMOS SPEAKS AT THE RICHMOND STREET EXIT   *Ben Volman*

Prepare to meet
thy God
—bump—
the highway off ramp
cut off the old brick church
at the brow
so they put up that sign
to meet your eyes:
and didn't changed it
for years.

Why not
prepare to be kissed by God?
prepare to enjoy your God?
prepare for cosmic love?
or
Don't prepare—let God surprise you.

Old Amos, shaking his fist
over the northern border
to Shiloh didn't pull threats out of a can:
he threw that wild, high yell
in a last act of mercy
while armies were dressing in steel
before dipping the sword into his people's blood
crying, "It's coming!
"You proud idiots behind your 12 foot walls,
"It's coming.
Every damn thing ye fear most
and it'll be thunder in yer hair
and fire in yer shoes,
plowing up yer cities like garbage
flung before a storm."

So,
d'ya wanna talk about mercy?
or is there a new prophet waiting
behind that sign
with a cocked Bible
for just the right sinner
to come over that rise
and let fly

JONAH'S WHALE ADDRESSES THE ALMIGHTY   *Laurie Klein*

Ruler of oceans, who can fathom
your summons? Pity my moans,
this small throat aching for everyday air.
Doubts are lice. They eat into brain and heart.
With a word, I'm consigned to an unknown shore.
Oh, maker of magnificent tails, reconsider
stranding me, far from the circle of my kind!
By your gift, salt is my song; your call
unleashes this sonar lament.

Never mind. You command my breath, as ever,
so let the columns of bubbles
rise, like prayers, our net
to enfold a wayward son. I'll do as I'm told, only
ease the lung-numbing gulp, the intestinal hell.
Then, may whatever end you design
close its mouth over me.
Not to leap, not to swim—but this I ask—
let me sink into you, before beaching.

BEFORE THE WIND *Laurie Klein*

High on mulled air, the bos'n stands lookout,
alive to salt, alert to wing and wind, the tang of land,
when starboard, the tempest arises,
driving a city of waves—
                    Avast! he cries.
                                      Stern to hull,
timbers groan. Jettisoned cargo sunders the whitecaps.
Sailors pray, and the pacing captain bellows for Jonah,
hammocked below,
        lost in nightmare:
                                a whale's gaping lip
like a swamped skiff, fringed with kelp. With a heave
she breaches, and that sighted coal in its socket,
that eye like an oven burns, turns on the dreamer with
lasic force.
        Shaken awake, Jonah quails
                                  at the captain's shout.
The gale howls. Lots are cast, Leviathan keens below
as God's fugitive kneels at the rail. "Out," he cries.
"Here is God's unholy bride:
                all is lost,
                        for I am chosen."

JONAH BEGINS TO THINK LIKE A PROPHET *Todd Davis*

When the words of the story swam near the shore,
I did not expect them to swallow me. And here
in the belly of this great fish made of language,
I am carried through green waters, scales pressed
tight, fins guiding me toward the depths of some
other tale. It is the creator of that story, who himself
was made by the sounds that issue from the throats
of my people, collected and drawn in black upon
the backs of leaves, then hidden away in a place
they call holy—it is that creator who tells this fish
where to swim and leaves me in the dark where words
begin to rot. Because I am hungry and cannot see, I say
fire and cook the word for bluefish and eat, satisfied
to wait in the orange reflection of my fear and the fire
that burns near it. Soon the person who will read
my story, who will speak the word and lay me face down
upon the beach, will enter this room and pick up this book.
And it is then I will collect white and gray and black
stones, take them into the center of town, let them fall
from my mouth. Because whether they are words
or stones, they will crush these people who do not believe
just the same.

RELUCTANT PROPHET   *Luci Shaw*

Both were dwellers
in deep places (one
in the dark bowels
of ships and great fish
and wounded pride,
the other
in the silvery belly
of the seas). Both
heard God saying
"Go!"
but it was the whale
who did as he was told.

RIB CAGE

Luci Shaw

Jonah, you
and I were both signs
to unbelievers.

Learning the anatomy
of ships and sea animals the hard way—
from the inside out—you counted
(bumping your stubborn head)
the wooden beams and the great
curving bones, and left your own heart
unexplored. And you were tough.
Twice, damp but undigested,
you were vomited. For you
it was the only way out.

No, you wouldn't die.
Not even burial softened you
and, free of the dark sea prisons,
you were still caged in yourself—
trapped in your own hard, continuing rage
at me, and Nineveh.

For three nights
and three days dark as night—as dark
as yours—I charted the innards
of the earth. I, too, swam
in its skeleton, its raw underground.
A captive in the belly of the world
(like the fish, prepared by God)
I felt the slow pulse at the monster's heart,
tapped its deep arteries, wrestled
its root sinews, was bruised
by the undersides of all
its cold, bony stones.

Submerged, I had to die, I had
to give in to it, I had to go
all the way down
before I could be freed to live
for you and Nineveh.

RAGE
Lynn Domina

His meals he flavored with chives, garlic,
green olives to scent his breath
with bitterness, though still he feared
he reeked—fingernails, hair, every pore
oozing the oily aroma of that great fish.

Rocked in its dark belly, he dared
God: abandon me forever. Abandon me

to this magnificent
stench. So the monster
spewed him into salted air, and Jonah
preached repentance in Nineveh, and God
received repentance from Nineveh and repented
of his own fierce anger. Jonah waited, eager
for ash to cascade upon the city, for sharp smoke
to suffocate it, for its very stones
to sizzle into new flame.

Soft rain stroked the air; clover
blossomed out of season. Jonah trudged

home, scrubbed himself through fiercely silent years,
his wife pacing the circumference of their well. Finally
she shouted he stank of nothing
but rage.

DRY BONES

Lynn Domina

Ezekiel 37:1–14

Ezekiel balances the rib
on his fingertip, comforted
by its parabolic curve, its regular
swing. Stepping left or right,
he crushes ankles, jaws, vertebrae, scatters
heaps of bleached bones. This rib—
perhaps a man's, one who loved
pottery or weaving, perhaps
a dog's or goat's. This skull
tipping onto his foot an infant's,
small as his palm, flattened,
toothless, dead before it could nuzzle
its mother's breast, hear her hum
evenings as dusk wavered
through their valley. Ezekiel imagines

a woman's forearm
supporting her child's spine,
sees her fingers nesting in his curls.
He considers the command: prophesy,
raise them up, each one
wondrous and living, thick
with flesh and desire. Ezekiel sees

the infant grow, squirm from his mother's lap,
tag after his tall cousin. He grows
until his arms and calves bulge
and then curls his hand
around a spear and thrusts it
into the drunk's heaving chest, cutting short
such stuporous slander.

No. He murders no one, this infant
squalling back at Ezekiel who prophesies,

promising sinews and skin
and spirit. The plain dampens
with drizzle. Bones heave upright,
stagger into their sockets, clashing
one into another like mallets,
like truncheons. Ezekiel covers
his ears, squints his eyes
against bewildered rage, these creatures
revived with the promise of another
death, their ears alert
to distant howls,
wolves already pausing
to sniff pungent flesh.

DANIEL TO THE CHIEF OF THE EUNUCHS — *Paul J. Willis*

But Daniel resolved that he would not defile himself with the king's rich food, or with the wine which he drank. . . . Daniel 1:8

No such food or wine
cross these lips of mine,
though the king may dine
   richly still.

Vegetables and water
keep your head from slaughter;
kingdoms feed and totter
   in their swill.

He of times and seasons
gives beyond our reasons,
nourishes and wizens
   whom he will.

Trust in God Most High:
temple is no sty.
Undefiled, I
   eat my fill.

THE FOURTH MAN   *Marjorie Maddox*

His face is the greater flame
but doesn't flicker. No furnace
fuels his glory. "Son of gods,"
the king calls out and cowers from the heat.
Sparks crown our heads.
We are un-singed and sing of seraphs,
genuflect before his servant,
ten times as golden as any man-made
Hades that can't consume
the luminous, the purified,
the once-upon-a-time burning bush,
the evermore-ignited blaze
of Yahweh.

EZRA 4 — *Debbie Sawczak*

(or, Samaritans Offer to Help Returned Exiles
Rebuild the Temple and are Rebuffed)

Were they really enemies—
those northerners nearby,
left like brash
behind Assyria's receding wave
to drive off squatting tribes
and keep the land from going wild?

Weren't they also Jacob's sons
whose forebears fretted at Sinai's foot
with yours,
covered their ears and begged
that God be silent?
Your great-great-great-grandparents said
the same glib yes to all his laws,
transgressed with similar aplomb,
and crowned and killed your kings,
oppressed your poor,
and danced round idols' altars
just like theirs did.
And pagan hosts abased and broke you, too,
when Yahweh judged.

Were you so pure, then—
back from Babylon—
too pure to let Samaritans lend a hand,
so sure that God commissioned
only you
to build his house again?
So what if they were Yahweh-seekers sacrificing
all this time in waiting—so they said.
They were not you, and you knew you
were better.

No wonder they were bitter,
writing letters to the bureaucrats
against you,
making trouble and red tape.

You won't forget that.

CHOIR PRACTICE

Nellie deVries

*...the singers had built villages for themselves
around Jerusalem.* Nehemiah 12:29

As she stirred the stew
she began the melody.

Next door, one was baking bread;
she blended in harmony.

Deep baritone rose from a third home,
as a hammer beat the tempo.

Voices joined from all the dwellings
till the whole choir was praising

and everywhere the children played
and swayed in cadence
with the song.

ANNOUNCEMENT   *Luci Shaw*

    Around his feet the air unfurls like flame.
    His burnished garments and his clarion voice
        Arouse her terror, yet she has no choice
        But welcome him. Gabriel, (his name—

God's Strength) accomplishes the age-long dreams
    Visioned by all Israel's virgins—that the One
    Borne from her youth was planned to be her own
        Since earth's foundations. Now it seems

    The ancient prophets' words are coming true
    (*Praise!*) and her life as Mother of God's Child
    Foretold. And so, how perfect are his words
    Of sudden salutation, *"The Lord is with you!"*

MARY CONSIDERS HER SITUATION   *Luci Shaw*

What next, she wonders,
with the angel disappearing, and her room
suddenly gone dark.

The loneliness of her news
possesses her. She ponders
how to tell her mother.

Still, the secret at her heart burns like
a sun rising. How to hold it in—
that which cannot be contained.

She nestles into herself, half-convinced
it was some kind of good dream,
she its visionary.

But then, part dazzled, part prescient—
she hugs her body, a pod with a seed
that will split her.

WONDER

Julie L. Moore

Amazing love! How can it be? —Charles Wesley

How did you do it?
Your disappearance
from glory, your break
into humanity?
                  Did you let the Father
scoop splendor from you
till you were hollowed
like heaven when you left?
How did the scraping go?
And how much did it hurt?
                          Or did the Spirit put you
under, tell you when you'd awake
you'd be good as new,
like the silk-spun skin
of a baby born that day?
No pain because you wouldn't know,
not yet, what you'd let go?
                      How did eternity
squeeze itself into the folds
of fat in your thighs,
how did all that light
funnel itself into your bones,
how did your breath, this time,
fill your own lungs?
                And how
did your open hands
furl into tiny fists,
fists you'd never shake at the skies?

GOD TRIES ON SKIN

Marjorie Maddox

Once, he stretched skin over spirit
like a rubber glove,
aligning trinity with bone,
twining through veins,
till deity square-knotted flesh.

In a whirlwind spin,
he shrank to the size of a zygote,
bobbed in a womb warm as Galilee's shore.

In the dark,
he brushed up on Hebrew,
practiced his crawl.

After months scrunched in a circle,
he burst through his cellophane sac,
bloodied the teen legs
spread on the straw.

In his first breath,
he inhaled the sweat
of Romans casting lots,
sniffed the wine mixed with gall.

DUMBSTRUCK   *Christine H. Boldt*

Zechariah said to the angel, "How will I know that this is so?'
Luke 1:18a NRSV

Zechariah, tending fires of incense,
You're frightened by Gabriel's sudden visit.
Good News is not always pleasant is it?
Who sent this word? Does it make any sense?
Should you say, "Welcome," or prepare your defense?
Are you touched by God? Have you lost your wit?
Aged priest tending the fires of incense,
You mistrust the angel's sudden visit,
Counting pledges of answered prayer nonsense
For an old man, an old woman, neither fit.
You temporize, reluctant to submit.
I, too, inquire, "What's the evidence?"
Even as I stoke altar fires with sweet incense.

VISITATION QUARTET
Annabelle Moseley

Luke 1:39–49

In one embrace: Elizabeth and John—
Jesus and Mary. As the women met,
two pregnancies entwined. Their men looked on.
God's instruments bowed, in a string quartet.
Their wombs, like violins, held pulsing song.
The baptist leapt in joy—the savior trilled.
And cello-like, Elizabeth's voice, strong,
gave blessing for belief that was fulfilled.
As a viola, Mary's psalm sustained.
Her harmony, a humble inner voice,
enraptured as it echoed. Wild—trained
in grace, gave their unborn call to rejoice.
It was both canticle and battle cry,
Sonata of surrender—lullaby.

THE NATIVITY
Annabelle Moseley

Luke 2:6–7

"She gave birth," Scripture says. One line to tell
of Mary's sacrifice. A mother knows
how much that means— the way each tiny cell
within each muscle feels a labor's throes.
And yet a mother wills the searing pain.
Her suffering allows her dear one birth.
And through a mother's long, heroic strain,
she focuses upon the gift's great worth.
Mary's libation, offered up to God
presented love through body, soul and will.
She felt him near, she almost felt him nod.
For through Christ's passion, God's word would fulfill—
through water and through blood, deliver all
to life—pushing through Calvary's grim caul.

ON THE ADORATION OF THE SHEPHERDS *David Brendan Hopes*

God is born tonight in the next town.
Be serious. Who wouldn't go?
Lock the back door. Turn the furnace down.
Throw a handful of food at the dog. Blow
off the dinner with the couple you really like.
Riffle through the bills for those
which absolutely will not wait. Take a hike.
The way? The consequence? The point? Who knows?
Select a path, an avenue, goat trail, a turnpike,
on through the twilight and the early snows.
Angel voices are, of course, a plus,
but go in dark and silence if you must.
Remember to seek the narrowest wretched door.
Prepare to diminish, resign, dispense, adore.

VISITING THE HOUSE OF BREAD

John B. Lee

We cross the border on our Israeli tour bus
briefly surrender our passports
to the no-Jews-welcome guards
and enter the little Palestinian town of Bethlehem
where in the dying time of Ovid's Roman gods
Mary came, arriving
with her swollen womb

I walk
the mistled streets
at a green-thorned hour
all holly-berry and agog
with a hot summer throng
of crèche vendors
with the angel-heralded child
carved out in olive wood
everywhere the camel-busy
carvers sit chiseling out a thirsty
caravan so we might stop and buy
a varnish-fragrant Balthazar
or make wise bargains
for the hammered-brass haloes of Byzantium
aglow about the forehead of the burning boy
not yet the carpenter
not yet the upstart rabbi
of a rebel cause
nor yet the martyr on his bloody cross
there in the barley dross
there in the grotto
of a water-silvered stone
we gawk at the famous carol-haven
near the nave
plod past that natal agony
we jostle shoulders for a better look
a hundred tourists mobbing
for a better look

and I am wondering
what has this day to do
with the innkeeper
turning his dung fork
in the donkey straw

on Christmas Eve at home
it often snowed
that cold surrender coming down
outside in angel-white around
the aromatic candle snuff
of church
and in my little coat
I took my mother's hand
and felt warm faith
beyond the door that I remember
slipping closed
on that unlasting light of youth
before imagination darkened down to wick scorch
on the winter-blackened sky

UNFINISHED

Nellie de Vries

*after Simeon in the Temple,
Rembrandt, 1669*

Fingers stretch
as if supplicating hands
are interrupted —
the answer placed
in his waiting arms.

Light glistens on his temple—
the mind consoled
by consolation's burden.

Death takes the prophet;
takes the artist
before his painting is complete;
takes the one
already bearing sin's stripes.

So certain are the words
"It is finished."

EPIPHANY

Laurie Klein

Perhaps, rolled in papyrus
or raw silk,
the jeweled boxes arrive as small thuds,
and gifts imprint the dirt floor.
Were the Magi
quiescent?—a hint of Quaker,
a nod to Zen—with nothing
verbal to treasure or
ever replay in their minds
save eloquent exhalations:
the creak of joints,
be they camels or kings,
the serial tick of straw.

For the marveling patience
of plastic wise men
en route, step-by-step,
to Mother's crèche (despite
my down-the-stairs drop kicks,
behind her back), I reposition
my knees, atoning, wordless
now, as the star comes for me.

MARY REMEMBERS FINDING JESUS IN THE TEMPLE

Annabelle Moseley

Luke 2:41–51

What joy it was to see his face again,
to feel his arms around me as I clung.
His eyes were like a merciful amen,
reflecting how mere days without him stung.
The storm was over now. Our fear was stilled.
Jesus invited us to walk across
the ocean of acceptance that he willed.
He knew someday he'd die upon the cross,
and did not want for us to wonder where
his soul had gone. This test had been our sign.
His loved ones could mourn, weep— but not despair.
He was not gone, but held by the divine—
about his Father's business for three days.
Trust. Even in a loss, God must be praised.

THE FORERUNNER   *Sandra Duguid*

Like the son
of struck dumb
Zacharias
our best words
cry in the wilderness

And come unseemly dressed
confusedly subject
to metaphor

John
of the camel's hair and leather
was not
that Lamb
that Light
that Word

So, for his preambling
paradox did:
after me
a follower
comes before

And cosmic irony:
Jordan man
revealing
the sponsor of the Holy Ghost
and fire

Allegorization:
the groomsman joys
to hear the bridegroom's voice

Oh, symbol-form grow great,
oh, symbol
less

'Til lovely
(as in pauses)

The Word
makes flesh
transcend itself

And John
his dearest speaker knows
what death it is to call
for priests and kings

So execution strikes—

But benediction
He comes
a blaze on water
Breath, on wings

JORDAN RIVER

Luci Shaw

Naaman went down seven times.
Imagine it—the leperous skin coming
clear and soft, and the heart too.
But can you vision clean Jesus
under Jordan's water? John the Baptizer did,
holding the thin white body down,
seeing it muddied as any sinner's
against river bottom, grimed by
the ground of his being.

Rising then, he surfaced, a sudden
fountain. But who would have expected
that thunderclap, the explosion of light
as the sky fell, the Spirit seizing him,
violent, a whirr of winged light and sound
witnessing his work, his worth,
shaking him until the drops
flew from his shoulders, wet and common
and holy, baptized sprinkling Baptizer.

MYSTERIOUS WAYS   *Paul J. Willis*

"They have no wine," his mother said to him.
He rolled his eyes. "Not now," he whispered. "Mom,
please." She didn't care about his secrets.
Why bear the Son of God if all he does
is keep it to himself? Here was a time
to make the promise good—and please the neighbors.
"Forget it. Absolutely not. You don't
have any idea what you're asking me.
Woman, no." And he rebuked her with
a godlike gaze. But mildly she turned
and told the servants, "What he tells you, do."

NICODEMUS'S COMPLAINT
Todd Davis

Wind steps heavy on us.
Trees tilting. Grass tossed.
A muddy green scroll
impossible to read.

I know the soul is a knot
of limbs, a ripple
on the river's surface.

Eventually light disappears
and stars go out. Even
the waters must recede
after the rainy season.

The body is pushed out
of a woman once, soul
broken and scattered.

How can anyone enter
the womb a second time?
And why won't you speak plainly
of the kingdom to come?

CONFESSION   Julie L. Moore

Mark 5:24–34

And in the twelfth year, there was still
    blood. And so many difficult degrees

of separation. Everything, at this point,
    burned. The once-soft skin of her labia.

The pathetic pulp of her womb.
    And the mass of hard questions.

Pressing on her like the crowds
    bearing down on him.

She knew the rules: Keep your hands
    to yourself. Whatever you touch you foul.

But she reached for him anyway.
    Fastened her un-

clean fingers, tipped
    with outrageous nerve,

onto the lip of his cloak.
    While he sensed the tug

of the siphon, the precious liquid of his power
    tapped, she felt her river of red

drain, the fierce spear of her pain
    withdraw.

He wanted to know who grasped
    such scandalous and particular

faith. Never again would she soil
    a place where she lay. So she fell

at his feet. Confessed.

MERCY
Christina Lee

John 8

A mob is one animal.
So many teeth in one mouth
snapping rage.

I cannot make myself
a mirror:
make them face it.

I can only dissolve
into their anger,
wait for the crush of it
and the weightlessness.

———

How they turn,
tuck-tailed,
snarls stuffed
back down throats.

Some hunch
as if tethered now
to stones they still hold.

How he takes from me
even my name.
He stands me up
and sends me out
with the rest of them.

LINES

Julie L. Moore

Scrawling on the very earth he created—
figure 8s? words? the fearful face

of the woman before him?—
the Christ fielded questions

about the fate of the adulteress.
It was a set-up. He knew that.

So he drew lines,
his index finger

pointing to the dust
they were subject to.

This far and no farther.

THE MAN BORN BLIND SENT TO SEE *Lynn Domina*

He recalled his mother's frustration
explaining transparency. *You see
through it*, she'd said, but he could discover
no pattern—wind though not smoke,
oil but not its lamp, not milk but water,
some demons only.

So here in the pool at Siloam, he stooped
to water cooling his feet, his ankles. He could see
water, its ripples, its eddies, and he could see
objects shining inside the water, stones,
clumps of mud, tawny weeds.
He could see his face,
frightening as magic, floating
inches below the surface. When he bent
to touch his beard, his finger
sank right through.

His hand leapt back into air
where he could see lines
at his knuckles, thin scratches, blue veins
curving to his wrist; yet still he saw
his hand's image where his hand
was not. This would be his joy

he understood, always seeing
more than was there.

TO LIVE ON

Angelina Schellenberg

Why
is she down
to her last coin?

Did no one speak
when the teachers of the law took
her husband's tools, her home?
Does no one call her
sister, neighbor, friend?

Has no one eyes
to see her and say
*she is our past,
my future*?

Why
does no one reach for
her trembling hand before
her last coin
drops

and after
she has given her all
to patch these ancient
stones,

will you
let her walk away?

MEMORIALS

Sandra Duguid

Yes, I indulged the moment:
setting my white heirloom box
next to his plate
at Simon's dull table;
placing my hand on his hair
to anoint his head with ointment—
the room awoke, wavered
in perfume.

His friends complained:
"Extravagance."
But how could I have spread thin
what ounce of wealth I owned?
I had watched this man
heal the blind and maimed,
heard him speak--
I was making amends for my doom.

And his, he said,
though I wasn't foreseeing a burial—
I've yet to understand;
we all die, I mean—eventually,
collapse,
we towers
of bone.

PRESENT   *Violet Nesdoly*

Luke 10:38-42

Mary's rapt attention
is her present to Jesus.
Though kitchen's clatter
bang, scrape and pour
together with multi-tasking Martha's
deep and pointed sighs
make the present tense
Mary chooses to stay
present, focused, listening
to Jesus present life—
unwrap past, present
and future.

MARTHA'S TROUBLE   *John Terpstra*

Martha was distracted by her many tasks... —Luke 10

I am caught in the trap of myself
Not a place I want to be
Do you not care?
Help me

You cannot help me
I am trapped in the snare
      of my own making
by my own doing

What have I done? Nothing
Everything
      Here, this tray, take one
from the many things I have been anxious over

Unburden me

I want out
I want not
to serve
      you, them, these hours
that pass like minutes to you all

minutes in which I feel myself aging

I want not to serve
         this need
this cup I drink

Who will take it from me?

HOW TO GO LIKE LAZARUS
Annabelle Moseley

I.
But what is in the way is always death.
The women dance, Lazarus, as you rise
among the bones, and then you take a breath
for the first time. Reborn, adjust your eyes
to filter light. Why fight it? All the skulls
around you smile. The rock is rolled away
from your tomb's entrance. Children shriek like gulls
and cry and laugh to see the stale bouquet
of you, dried flowers falling from your hands.
But all is beautiful to you. You see
each corpse around you rising, understand
the future, suddenly. And you foresee
skin wrapping around bones, the awkward dance
of resurrection, of a second chance.

II.
And when the scales fall, you can see your prize.
Your burial bands drop—your fish's scales.
For days you swam in nothingness, your eyes—
unseeing shells, and now the seaweed veils
have sunk down deep below. You've risen toward
the surface, to new life. You are untied
from shrouds of kelp. You breathe and are restored.
Your name is Lazarus, you rode the tide
of death to life. You'll die again someday.
But living is the art that you prefer.
Each time is better than the last, a way
to fight the masochist, the saboteur,
the voice inside that's taunting, casting stones—
because you want to dance among the bones.

ON THE ROAD FROM JERUSALEM
Christina Lovin

I would recognize any one of them anywhere now,
that band of thieves who surrounded and attacked me.
I memorized every one of their faces
and knew it was more than my money they wanted.

That band of thieves who surrounded and attacked me
on the road from Jerusalem to Jericho
knew it was more than my money they wanted:
It is his apparel that gives a man away

On the road from Jerusalem to Jericho
I lay wounded and naked in a roadside ditch.
It is his apparel that gives a man away:
it's easy to recognize a priest by his robes—

I lay wounded and naked in a roadside ditch
and that man passed to the other side of the road.
It's easy to recognize a priest by his robes:
for yet another man was traveling that day, as well,

and that man passed to the other side of the road,
but not before I could fully see his face.
Yet another man was traveling that day, as well:
he looked down at me and gave me his hand

before I could fully see his face.
Me, naked and shivering in a ditch and
he looked down at me and gave me his hand,
lifted me up and covered me with his own blanket.

Me, naked and shivering in a ditch, and
there were three men who passed that way: the third
lifted me up and covered me with his own blanket,
the second was a Levite, the first, a priest—two religious men.

There were three men who passed that way. The third

was a Samaritan—my supposed enemy. And the other two?
The second was a Levite; the first, a priest—two religious men.
Then there was the band of thieves.

A Samaritan—my supposed enemy, and the other two
(I memorized each of their faces),
and then there was the band of thieves.
I would recognize any one of them anywhere now.

A LONG WAY OFF

Laurie Klein

Owing consumes
all but hunger.
           Pride,
with its broken tusks,
roots among the rinds
and gristle, half-gnawed,
the trough of water,
                fouled.
Twigs mirror my fingers,
a snack for the great sow's heat:
the snuffling maw, those rank
hooves. Mired
                    amid the forbidden,
luck is one corner, behind a rock,
a thorn bush for warmth.
                I am
dreaming of veal. Dates. A chalice
beside a bowl,
            the bruised seed
oiled and kneaded—see it rise,
steaming, then torn.
              Mile by mile
the stones mock. these cracked feet
curl, as if dead to my father, leaving
a trail, blood and husks. Each apology
rehearses me,
            running on and on.

LEAVING PARADISE
(LAZARUS TO THE RICH MAN)

Cameron Alexander Lawrence

Luke 16:19–31

Why do you sit there hunched? Every chasm has two sides.
Here tree limbs are fruit heavy, the water cold and pure.

How slim you look now, no longer draped in folds of linen.
When you passed on the street, I reached up as if begging a sun

or some radiant planet for particles of light, fleeting warmth.
I was the small moon pulled into hope of another orbit.

Evenings, when the dogs came in darkness, I could hear music
through open windows, food and wine pouring on wind—

the laughing women and moneyed men who danced
with them: a kind of heaven visible only from the outside.

Do you not recognize me now that my muscles are full,
skin taut once again like a young man's? Death brought me here.

Now I know you remember—your face answers for you.
But be at peace: I have already forgotten which of us hated whom.

I see you are cold, old friend, that you continue to mold
your fingers into a bowl and sip them. Forgive me,

there is no way to give you drink, no bridges this side of time.
Where even the angels are held back from leaving paradise.

JESUS THE CHRIST—BEFORE A MEAL

Richard Osler

Walk while you have the light
just a little while longer.
John 12:35

On the cedar wood, distressed and worn,
light slips sideways,
too fast
to be caught. Even by me.
First word. Last word.
Caught in time. Timeless. Tired
of paradox. The light, I remember,
I illumined and threw into a darker
dark, catches me
by surprise and I can't grasp it
here. I, who am
light. But the darkness doesn't
believe it.

Knows it
not.

THE LORD JESUS ON
THE NIGHT HE WAS BETRAYED

Debbie Sawczak

1 Cor. 11

The Lord Jesus on the night he was betrayed took,
broke, gave to his disciples
himself, and bread.
A stylist protests
the syntactic interruption,
the six-word subordinate clause fixed snug
between subject and verb,
so to be received and recited forever.
But as with so many endeavours,
here timing is everything.
on the night he was betrayed:
on the night he sat next to treachery,
bathed the feet of his enemy,
shared his bowl;
the night the elders of his sanctified tribe
hissed stratagems,
assembled torches and weapons;
the night our humanity's venom rose,
flowed over our brim
to rid us of him
and drown that heaven's hound's love.
On that night of shattered covenant!
That was the night he gave twelve turncoats
himself, torn, as blessed bread
and warming, mending wine
instead.

THE AGONY IN THE GARDEN *Annabelle Moseley*

Matt 26:36–39

Within a garden like this we were lost.
Eden was rooted to Gethsemane—
We slept while you kept watch and mourned the cost—
gazing at moonlight through the olive trees.
Your red drops fell, consoling Abel's blood
which once cried out from deep within the earth.
Your tears and sweat baptized and blessed the mud.
Sacrificed slumber would have had great worth.
You'd barred us from nightmares: forbidden fruit
we tasted in our dreams. You gave true bread.
We could have nourished you, provided shoots
of strength for branch-deep weariness. Instead,
we closed our eyes, with everything at stake.
All we'd been asked to do was stay awake.

JESUS MIGHT HAVE
Luci Shaw

Jesus might have died
a dozen times before he died.

An incidental death--tetanus
from a nail, a splinter.

A drowning at baptism.
A drink from a tainted well.

Rotten fish.
Desert thirst.

A stoning, a getting
pushed over the edge,

or overboard in a storm.,
A choking by a demon on the loose,

a bar room brawl
in the local pub.

So when it happened, it seemed
like someone finally

got it right. For God to let it
happen.

SONG OF GOD: FOR JUDAS NOT YET BORN

Barbara Colebrook Peace

to bring up the horizon in relief as clay under a seal,
until all things stand out like the folds of a cloak,
when the light of the Dog-star is dimmed
and the stars of the Navigator's Line go out one by one.
— Job 38:14,15 New English Bible

Judas, sprawled on the grass, the sun in your eyes as you look up
and laugh, plucking a stalk and whistling between your green-stained
thumbs, saying *This is better than Jerusalem.*
Judas, child of lostness, how could I bear it
if you were not born?
Your features known to me in every detail.
How could I not bring you to birth, when even now
clouds passing over the earth part to reveal
your face in shadow between fire and starlight; even now the daystar
    awaits my signal
to bring up the horizon in relief as clay under a seal,

and the angels, who have thousands of different words for light,
have arranged the light around you.
In our little camp on the mountain slope,
Peter and James and John are still asleep;
only you and I stay awake to see the dawn,
our clothes smelling of lentil stew and woodsmoke.
We have stayed up talking, you and I, all night.
Now we wait for the woods and valleys to slowly emerge,
and the long mountain ridges unfold in their beauty, one by one,
    picking up the sun's spark,
until all things stand out like the folds of a cloak,

the earth in this moment unique; only you and I share.
We are not ready to come down from the mountain.
The wind is passing over the house where you will be born.
If you are not born I could not bear it.
Before we go down from the mountain, we tell each other

what we dreamed:
you dreamed your mother dying
and you tell me your greatest fear:
being left alone at the time of death, no sound of human voice, only
   the wind,
when the light of the Dog-star is dimmed.

It is Sabbath, and the morning of your birth. *Shalom, Judas,*
peace be with you;
the earth rising on the first morning of the earth,
fragile blue jewel, my beloved Judas.
Peter and James and John are still asleep.
It is time to come down from the mountain.
Will you remember this, will it be enough to keep you from
despair, when you greet me with a kiss as the men come
bearing torches,
                  and the last word I speak to you on earth is
  Shalom—
and the stars of the Navigator's Line go out one by one?

MARY MEETS JESUS ON THE WAY OF THE CROSS

Annabelle Moseley

And there followed Him a great multitude of people, and of women, who bewailed and lamented him. Luke 23:27

When he was not yet two, he hurt himself.
He found his father's bench, climbed up the rail,
and reaching for a hammer on the shelf,
he pricked his finger on a sharpened nail—
and cried out. Holding him, I was dismayed
to see four beads of blood fall to the ground.
Between torment and love, my spirit swayed.
Each drop looked like a red rose petal— round
and bright. This, just his first wound, still I longed
to gather every floret of his pain
because it was a part of him, belonged
inside the reliquary of his veins
or washed by God-sent rain or shared, adored.
In each drop was an endless vineyard stored.

In each drop was an endless vineyard stored.
And as he staggered toward me with the cross,
seeing his gaping wounds, the blood that poured,
hearing the women wailing for my loss,
my heart quickened and opened like a rose
in torment and in love, to take each thorn
they crowned him with into myself— enclose
each trace of lost blood, pain. Since he was born,
I knew this day would come. I didn't know
that as our eyes met, I would see the child
that he had been, those many years ago.
I tell you, as he caught my eyes, he smiled—
through pain, to comfort me. His march resumed—
and each red drop he shed anointed, bloomed.

SIMON OF CYRENE   *Mary Lee*

Feet trample, horses neigh,
crowd strains.

Terse Roman soldiers control:
a hefty gloved hand on his shoulder –
he struggles against heavy grip;

The procession pauses.
A wooden beam descends,
he is no volunteer – a conscript.

Arms expand skyward
to steady the load. The procession
advances, he stumbles.

Irritation rises:
Jewish dignity recoils
under the foreign yoke.

The slope steep, his
stooped figure staggers.

Is his soul as dejected
as his bent back?

The sharp beam cuts
as he curses his people's
oppression. He falls –

the curse dies on his lips;
the bleeding farmer in from
the country that Friday is exhausted.

Now he hoists the wooden weight
and treads upwards.

VIA DOLOROSA

John B. Lee

I have walked
the walk of sorrow
those twelve stations
set within the walls of old Jerusalem
I have tasted the wine
and felt
the bitter kiss
I have trod the cobbled
rise and fall
of the city
like a sea of stone
I have worn
the barbed halo
of a thorny crown
and shouldered
the shadow's measure
of Rome's heavy cross
like bulling a post
into a hole I've dug
for a fence on the farm at home
I have seen the dark cavern
of last sleep
with the shape of a dream
etched in the old anatomy of rock

(an elderly pediatric nurse
told me only yesterday
of the dolorous event
of seeing the final impression
of a dead child's head
left behind
as a small dip
in the still-warm linen
of a pillow slip
not so deep
as a restless punch a sleeper might make

seeking comfort in cool feathers
and she wept
to have seen the weight of thought
like a raindrop plunged in sand)

and here the sign
to mark a wall
to say—see here's
a wall that is not there

the hollyhock
grow wild along the road
the oleander thrive
the bougainvillea
thicken gardens in the street
the orchards bloom and hum
the cypress and the olive
live and prosper where they stand
the common thistle
prick a purple breath
of weather
come to cool the hand
I see
the pulse points of my heart
they haunt my wrist
just where the soul is born
from nails
new light arrives
to pierce blue regions
of my blood
and heaven's grief
comes down in hammered gold
so thin it drifts
in shadowcast that leaves
no shadow where it falls

THERE IS NO TIME FOR LOVE TO BE BORN

Christine Valters Paintner

Aren't there annunciations / of one sort or another / in most lives?
— Denise Levertov

There is no time for love to be born
in a world flailing under fear,
trampled by terror, crushed by callousness.
There is no room for love to be born
under the heft of pressing grief,
no open portals in the perpetual busyness
or the list of endless tasks minted newly each morning,
where "to do" never seems to include "love more."
No opening in the jostled and tinseled shops,
which promise to soothe the ache and awfulness of our burdens.

I see you there holding your infant son, pink-scrubbed and new.
I see you there holding his grown dead body, brutalized and hollow.
Your sobs rumble protest as he is lifted from your arms,
longing to still be earth-tethered by the weight of blood and bones.

You are not orbiting the sun,
but instead the great dirge, swaying me from note to note,
the wailing daughter whose mother's heartbeat has just halted,
the river's cold splash when another one gives up,
the soldier's wound which sends him home,
the slivered crescent descending against a black horizon.
the winter's pale morning light streaming between dusty curtains,
the newly discovered constellation.
You are the birth mother and the death mother.

There is no time for love to be born,
only the willing descent into all the battered and frozen places,
the opening of doors long ago latched and rusted.

Comets slash the sky with warnings of direness.
You are the breaking open of star-streaked

cracks where woe loses its sturdy grip,
where in the most ordinary of moments,
when all else nudges us further toward despair,

suddenly we feel the wild impulse arising
to say yes.

THE DISCIPLE CRADLES IN HIS ARMS THE DEAD CHRIST

John Terpstra

after Caravaggio's Deposition, *or* Entombment

In the beginning, word was
    he's our man.
I do not believe in man.

From the moment he hauled us out of the water,
    out of our lives, our element,
we lived.
We were as fish who breathe air.

This plunges me back
into a reality I no longer believe exists.

He lies here in my arms
    at the bottom of the boat
asleep, while the sea and elements rage
    and we drown.

I no longer hear the heart
that beat so strongly in my ear
    the rhythm of love.

What is that smell?
Mary's ointment? The nard of her anointing
    his journeyed feet,
her hair the towel,
a scent that filled the corners of our home?
Or is it from the precious stuff
our friend has purchased
    to fill the nasals of the tomb?

A little while, he said.
And then a little while again, he said.
But all the books on all the shelves
    could not contain all that he said.

And I do not believe my eyes.
I do not believe the dark
dark enough
   to overpower,
though the light is out.

Although the light is out
we will place the light inside the hollowed rock.
We will set the light
 in death's open mouth,

and see.

JOSEPH OF ARIMATHEA *Marjorie Maddox*

Patron Saint of Funeral Directors

"His was my most important body,
the corporeal link to our souls,
rehearsal for resurrection. Yes,
he was dead. My tears pooled in his sores,
and when I wrapped each limb,
the little left of his blood
poured into the open prayer of my palms.
His torso, tattooed with that centurion's spear,
took more time and linen.
'My purse for a pulse,' I thought,
but knew his promise was better.
Except for the women and guards,
I took his body alone to the new tomb.
And then I waited."

THE BURIAL OF JESUS *Annabelle Moseley*

John 19:41-42

A grave within a garden, garden grave.
Tonight among the trees and ancient stone,
we planted him who faced the scythe to save,
we gave the root of Jesse, blood and bone.
Within a rock-hewn tomb, we placed the vine.
Though he was cut, he still bore every branch.
A place of rot and growth holds Jesus' shrine.
Here Eden's tears and blood, his grave will stanch—
for my son nourishes the earth's deep thirst.
Gethsemane received his blood as rain.
I long to follow him, the boy I nursed,
inside the cave to pacify my pain.
But that thought passes. Recollect his light.
I wonder where his soul's seed rests tonight.

MAGDALEN

Philip C. Kolin

Again tears reigned
In her eyes running
Ahead of the horizon.

She expected death—
Pressed linen in a sealed
Alabastered tomb,
The sad security of stone.

There before her
The laughter of angels
Sprung the snares of time.

Her life sighed
A history of touch
Her hair, his feet.

Who keeps a garden
In a grave?
Robbers, she thought.
As she turned

She saw the one
Whose caress
Would never feel
The same again.

JAMES THE LESS   *D.S. Martin*

In what way were you less?   Shorter
younger   shyer   than that son of thunder
who shared your name?   Not one to impress
or be given fame   or the one who came
later to the band?   Were you the same James
whose father was Alphaeus   the one whose mother
was a second Mary beneath the cross
the second mentioned among the women
at the tomb?   Would you confess
to taking the blame   to feeling the worst
to seeing yourself whenever he would bless
the least in the kingdom?   Step up James
claim your place   Remember he said
the last shall be first

INVITING A FRIEND TO SUPPER   *Paul J. Willis*

These hills show evening, the day is spent,
spent like lost coins spilled down a viper's hole,
like stumbling sheep too far from Jacob's well,
like blood run down a post, or down a spear
in some lost Roman cause, in Caesar's wars.
We walk in vain, and here we take our rest:
in this small village pause, remain with us.
You are some comfort in your wayward talk,
the little that you know an odd relief
to our large sorrow—pleasing to return
to our scrolled prophets. Moses, after all,
is our best hope and always was—how strange
we should have thirsted more. We shall be stones
planted by streams of water, by this brook
that runs beside Emmaus. Here, turn in.
We'll wash your feet, an upper room awaits—
you shall be served. Come, sir, break bread with us.

EMMAUS ROAD REMEMBERED
Luci Shaw

My camera's small eye waits to catch
and hold small chronicles of glint and shape
and shine. The subtle shadings in its
blunt black box all hold their breath until
a kind of resurrection happens on a screen.
An esoteric magic translates them into sharp details
to view again, and show to friends.

Trust needs to know that sounds and sights
and words imprinted later, tell the truth
about that couple, part of a holy triad
walking, listening, stopping for evening hunger.
Did they get it right when they remembered?
Was he a wishful phantom of their grief?
After the sudden vanishing did they play
with the crumbs, wondering? How carefully
did they gather up those husks,
memorials of loaf and life and resurrected bread?
And can we learn from them
to feast on mystery, taking a broken loaf
from the outstretched hand of the Unseen?

EMMAUS

Debbie Sawczak

I

I am packing my bundle for Emmaus.
We tried to postpone,
neither of us much in the mood anymore.
He was evidently just a passing messiah,
yet his passing has opened a pit at my feet.
I will fall in forever
if I dare a step.
Now and then,
I back up, wide-eyed,
ask myself, 'What
is that frozen manlike thing
that clenches a soul in its fist?'
And I answer:
'Oh, yes—it is me,
holding me.'

II

I hear things as if they were far away.
My brother Matthias's talk:
"Be good if it rains,
it'll settle the dust . . .
We should stop in the shade and rest,
do you think?
. . . I wonder what Uncle wants to talk to us about?"
Here I surprise myself by muttering,
"Not about God or the Promise, I hope,"
while I try by vigorous kicking
to get the pebble out of my sandal.

III

"Cleopas,"
says my brother.
Out of the corner of my eye he looked at me twice
before daring my name.
"They did say they'd seen him alive.
Alive.
What do you call that, Cleopas?
Dreams? Wishing?"
The sun glitters hard like a shield,
like a new coin over our heads,
and gilds the roof of the roadside taberna.
"Probably both, Matthias;
anyway, the Romans are still in charge."

IV

Man comes up even with Matthias.
A face you might see any day in the market,
but a line of pocklike marks on the forehead,
dark eyes deeper than Jacob's well.
He doesn't strike me as a robber,
but I've learned:
in this world, you don't know who anyone is.
I return his nod and look up the white rutted road,
see nothing in the glare.
"You two seem low;
wasn't your Passover happy?"
Staring, I stumble in surprise
and say,
"What?! And where have *you* been?"
The pebble rolls suddenly out of my sandal.
The untidy story spurts from my loosened lips.

V

The man is as good at prophecy as Jesus.
(I can't believe I am thinking that!)
But in his mouth the prophets are a riddle
whose answer,
increasingly suspiciously,
looks like Jesus:
this weekend from which I am reeling is really
the perfect, preposterous answer.
Unbearable knowledge crouched at my mind's edge
springs to the centre, explodes,
so hot it scorches my heart.
It smashes the scaffolding skillfully raised
round my crumbling spirit.
I am limp and dumb like a baby just out of the womb
before the first breath.

VI

Fortunately, as always,
Matthias can still use his tongue:
"We're here, our uncle lives just in here;
look, it's sunset,
stay with us, come,
we'll give you supper.
Sorry, we have no servant;
there's water in the jar
in the corner by the door
for your hands and feet."
Our guest glances meaningly at us,
then back at the jar;
his faint smile broadens, opens to a grin.

VII

I rap the bowls down quickly, wood on wood,
while Matthias stacks up questions:
"When will this kingdom of the Scapegoat start?
How, again, are we healed by his stripes?
What about 'coming on the clouds'?
What's that you said about the 'sign of Jonah'?

But Sir, if first you would say the blessing—?
We'll talk some more over food."

Man takes the bread in lean dark hands,
and lifts them.
I suddenly see those marks,
they deafen me one long moment,
I hear no word
till the Amen breathed
    as the bread is torn:
that sinewy twist I know!
I know that particular roll of the wrist,
am seeing it now for the sixtieth time
and the first.
My heart has burst!

And his chair is empty.

ST. PETER ON THE ETERNITY OF THREES

Philip C. Kolin

I learned that eternity unfolded in threes.
Mary told us stories of magi on dromedaries
and losing her son in the temple

but finding him three days later,
just as he found James, John, and me
and led us to that tabernacled mountain top.

Coming down we wiped the dazzle
from our eyes to see the multitudes
 spread like lilies across the fields.

We thirsted to return to the light.
But then came Gethsemane
and the bloody tears he shed

turned everything an opalescent red.
The priest's courtyard felt as cold
as my tongue; with each cock crow

the wind seared my soul.
I could not watch those crosses
going up or the temple veil

ripping apart. The darkness
that followed blazed my betrayal
like a comet warning doom.

On the third day the women
Salome, Joanna, Magdela
ran back from the tomb with the earth-

shaking news that he had risen,
his burial linens limp on the floor.
I dreamt I saw him

seated at the center of the table again,
above the clouds, moon, and stars,
feasting with a dove and a white-bearded patriarch.

THOMAS DIDYMUS   *D.S. Martin*

When Mary Magdalene   said she'd seen
the Lord   it was strangely disappointing
One of the worst women   saved from the street
to have been first   I knew it must be true
that's just what he would do   but then
when I was the only one   to fight fear
& search for myself   the others lagging behind
it was like the soldier's spear   went right through
me too   when I returned to hear
the others bragging   (that was the worst)
that I was the only one   not to have been there
not to have seen where his hands were pierced
I went into denial   *I won't believe*   I said
Anything less than my fingers in his wounds
won't be enough   My words sounded odd
to my ears   A week later I was among
them when he appeared   & called my bluff
My Lord & my God   Conviction rolled off my tongue

STORING UP TREASURE

Angelina Schellenberg

After Sarah Klassen's "Horizon"

It isn't easy to write a poem about
Jesus. One might describe his lean legs, soiled toes
trampling smooth stones, riding a wave,
his cheek turning to mark the hand that slaps,
fingers of clay reaching to cleanse cloudy eyes,
his eyes that see through skin to stiff neck, congested
heart beneath.

Perhaps a poem would reveal
stripes where his tunic should have been,
tears from breaking the fall, clearing a path
through the swords, thieves, and rust.
But could a poem capture
the sizzle of fish on the rock,
the woo of wind by his open side,
the laugh in his throat as he calls,
Have you caught anything?

JUDAS, PETER

Luci Shaw

because we are all
betrayers, taking
silver, and eating
body and blood, and asking
(guilty) is it I, and hearing
him say yes,
it would be simple for us all
to rush out
and hang ourselves.

But if we find grace
to cry and wait
after the voice of morning
has crowed in our ears
clearly enough
to break our hearts,
he will be there
to ask us each, again,
do you love me?

ALMOST APOSTLE   *Eric Potter*

Acts 1

Three years I followed the Rabbi,
left what life I had behind,
took to the road, no place to lay
my head nowhere to call my home.
My family called me crazy, said
I was shirking responsibility.
What a way to honor your mother
and me, my father said. My brother
just shook his head; my sisters, proud
of their husbands, solid men, whose beards
drip with oil, whose bellies swell
beneath rich tunics, warned I would
never marry. What decent family
would send a daughter to a man
who can't hold down a steady job?
What did I care for all those warnings?
Those three years were the best thing
that ever happened to me. For once
I was part of something, not of the three,
or even of the twelve, but not
so far from them as you might think.
Though I hung back, they knew my name,
and always I could make Peter laugh.

What could I say of those three years?
I saw it all: the sick made well,
the lame to walk, the blind to see.
I stuffed myself on fish and bread
till I could barely move, and sat
spellbound on sunny hills to hear
his words and couldn't get enough,
I held my breath when they broke the seal
on Lazarus's tomb, and gasped
in relief when he struggled forth.

It was my cloak beneath the master
when he sat the donkey, and I shouted
myself hoarse with the crowd that day
and wept myself dry when the soldiers
took him. I stayed on the edge,
too far away to see his back
in ribbons or the nails' rust,
but not so far I couldn't hear
his final cry or see the dark
descend I thought would never lift.

I heard the rumors. First the women,
then John and Peter. I chalked them up
to grief—I missed him, too, and thought
I saw him everywhere. Like all
the rest I took him for a ghost
until he took a bite of fish
and ate a bit of honeycomb.
I didn't need to see his hands.

O, I could say the things I saw,
but what I liked best was bedding down
beneath the stars. An early riser,
I tried to be a help, stirred up
the fire and watched the sky begin
to pink, the scattered sleepers spread
across the ground like Joseph's coat.

Some mornings Jesus would appear
as if from nowhere, his cloak heavy
with dew, his hair tangled, returned
from whatever quiet place he'd spent
the night, and join me round the fire.
I'd break off hunks of bread for us,
we'd hand the wineskin back and forth
and talk of everything we'd seen
the day before, what lay ahead,
and best of all the heft of tools

the scent of fresh cut wood.
He dearly missed them, I could tell,
could tell how he loved to work the wood
along the grain with patient strokes
as if to free its inner shape.

Some mornings he'd just stare into
the fire until the others stirred,
then he'd gather himself and rise,
laying his hand upon my shoulder—
a heavy hand, work-rough and strong—
he'd squeeze it once and move on.

And what could I truly say? I long
to hear that voice and feel that touch again.

THE THIRTEENTH APOSTLE   *Paul J. Willis*

And they put forward two, Joseph called Barsabbas, who was surnamed Justus, and Matthias. Acts 1:23

I thought I had a chance. Indeed I did—
fifty-fifty at the very least.
Judas, that was no surprise to me—
I'd seen him taking silver from the purse.
So when he burst upon his bloody field,
when Jesus came again and shortly left,
when we repaired en masse to the upper room
and prayed, and prayed, and prayed again some more,
'twas I who let a scrap of parchment fall
at Peter's side just when his eyes were closed.
I'd copied there a very pregnant line
from out the Psalms: "Let someone take his office—
someone else." And when his eyes he opened,
mine I shut, prostrating myself near
him in my plea for God's own Holy Spirit
to descend. But out the side of my
half-blinded eyes, I saw him take it up
and saw the light begin to dawn in his
dim fisher's mind. He had been waiting for
a chance like this, a way to throw about
his bossiness in some invented piece
of self-important business. "Brothers," he said,
"the Holy Scriptures now must be fulfilled
concerning Judas and his empty place."
And he went on much longer than was need.
I listened open-eyed, as if awaked
from deepest supplication, and his glance
soon fell on me—on me—on Joseph Justus,
the worthiest of all in that great room.
He was about to name me—to anoint me—
when that curst John came whispering in his ear
and pointed to Matthias by the door.
Matthias, he who'd hardly said a word

in three years' time of tramping in the dust.
'Twas he who was in charge of reefing sail
that night we nearly swamped in Galilee.
He lacked ambition, had no sailor's sense—
he'd almost drowned us all, and didn't care,
just hung on Jesus, moon-eyed as the rest.
But now the slate was named, and I employed
myself in rearranging some short speech
I long had contemplated for this time.
I cleared my throat, was humbly going to rise,
when Peter plunged the company perforce
into one of his interminable prayers.
"Lord, you can read the heart," he said, and paused—
"the heart of every man and woman here."
And then, instead of casting proper votes,
they held up straws picked off the filthy floor.
I was constrained to choose, and then Matthias.
Mine was the shorter; and I let it fall.
Amid the tongues of feigned congratulations,
I left that room and found the windy dark.
I only wish that someone yet remained
who would be worth my while to betray.

PENTECOST

Margo Swiss

And suddenly there came a sound from heaven
as of a rushing mighty wind, and it filled all
the house where they were sitting.
And there appeared unto them cloven
tongues as of fire, and it sat upon each of them.
—Acts 2:2–3.

She had dreaded it might come again
like the first time, with a ravishing,
often after startling up from sleep
at the felt-thought of it—

But here and now at nine in the morning
with all his wind and fire
that same God Almighty rush
swept through, broke open

every last petrified heart there
fine-tuned in a moment,
each an angel's harp humming
hymned holy with one accord—

She wept with the rest,
all eyes streaming, joyed to behold
one another's flame, hovering above,
like something with wings—

bustling to life a new song
choired together, tongues in chant
solemn weave of words:
one vast canopy spread over

a living table laid before them,
so lavish, so fair, where
all might sit and eat of nothing spoiled
with none unclean among them.

ANANIAS EXPLAINS THE SITUATION TO SAPPHIRA

Violet Nesdoly

Acts 5:1–11

We've got to be together on this story.
Our actual profit they don't have to know.
Peter's not that good with money, honey.
We'll keep some back for times when east winds blow.

This partial sum buys quite a reputation
equal and more to the full the others gave.
It's worth at least a plaque commemoration—
I'm sure our gift will follow us to the grave.

ANANIAS LAYS HANDS ON SAUL[6]

Todd Davis

The light, which left a scrim of salt
upon my skin, was speaking, and the voice

addressed me with the noise wind makes
in weeds or the drumming of bulrushes.

When it ceased, I could not see,
and my companions took me by the arms

into the city where in a room made of mudbricks
the voice returned, this time as ice and snow

strafed to the sides of leaves. For three days
I did not eat or drink, quiet as I considered

the pair of ravens that were my hands. Then,
another pair of hands, like the useless, forgotten

wings of a hen, touching the sides of my face,
and the scales, which were not like the snake's

sloughed skin but like the sheerest yellow petal
of the flower that grows near water's edge,

falling from my eyes and becoming dust.

---

6 The name Ananias, mentioned in these two poems, refers to two different men.

PHILIPPI   D.S. Martin

Acts 16

Lying in damp darkness every sound is magnified
the clink   clatter and scrape of dragged chains
the drip of distant water

The clop of donkey hooves approaches out in the street
fills this cold stone hole   & then slips away
like a rat through a crack

From deep in the inner cell   a tune begins
Two Jews   who've just been beaten   raise voices
in praise to their god

Such odd behaviour   that keeps us from sleep in this
hopeless place?   *His praise will continually
be in my mouth*

That's when the rumbling begins   dust & debris
earth quake   doors open   fetters break   & each of us
out in the moonlit courtyard

We are too stunned to run   as the wide-eyed jailer
rushes in   a trembling torch in his hand   flames flickering
on his astonished face

DWELLING

Nellie deVries

2 Corinthians 5; 2 Timothy 4

In a Roman prison
the tentmaker looks at his hands,
calloused and needle-pricked,
and remembers a metaphor he had written:
*...if the earthly tent we live in is destroyed,
we have a building from God, an eternal house
in heaven, not built by human hands.*

He shudders at the chill autumn winds
and groans, longing to be clothed
with his heavenly dwelling.
With cold-gnarled fingers he grabs a quill
and writes, *My dear son, I long to see you.
Bring my cloak, and my scrolls, especially
the parchments. Come to me quickly.
Do your best to get here before winter.*

PAUL'S THORN
Luci Shaw

*Therefore, to keep me from being conceited, I was given
a thorn in the flesh, a messenger from Satan....* 2 Cor. 12:7

Thorn—the word meaning
sharpened stake. Even as metaphor
it feels fierce. And simply to keep conceit
at bay? It seems a harsh mercy,
this gift sent from God via Satan—

Or was the Father saying, "Paul, this is
what happened to my Son, though
underserved. thorns crown-pressed
his forehead. A stake buried itself in his own side
and four spikes pinned his hands and feet
into the pulp of a wooden beam.

When Paul bragged a bit from time to time,
we wonder--where did God pierce him? Tooth?
Armpit? Groin? Naked sole? We speculate,
feeling for him, while owning our own
shortcomings. When my joints ache does it mean
I am conceited, and therefore called
to thank heaven for the infliction? But cancer,
and the baby, born after five failures
taken in his crib at four months. Thorns?

How to make sense of this, and how
to answer our perplexities? I've never
been hi-jacked to the third heaven, yet
may I learn to crop my secret self-
importance as a means towards discipline,
pain a divine endowment. If possible, I'll
put up with that sharp gravel in my sandal;
and a sore that will not heal. I'll ask:
Is it vexation, or disguise for grace?

WHAT JAMES DIDN'T SAY ABOUT THE TONGUE *Luci Shaw*

That it is almost prehensile, a pink
muscle manipulating morsels of fruit, of slander.
That you can feel it, right now, tensing
in your mouth as it scans the possibilities of tang.
That it probes with equal avidity the cavity left
where the filling fell out, and the heart
of the olive--toying with its little flag of pimiento.
That it obsesses over the sharp edge
of a chipped tooth or a canker in the cheek.
That it is aggressive in the sinuous frenzy
of a kiss, and athletic in its efforts to search beyond
the lips to nose, to chin, or narrow to a little
hovering snake head of pure investigation.
Restless, a blind, amphibious animal,
ceaselessly testing the limits of its porcelain cage,
cunning in shaping breath into word: half-truth
or proverb, benediction or blight.
As original as Eden. As unmanageable.

WANDERING STARS   *Ryan Apple*

after Jude

You will hardly notice it happening at first
so watch for the signs
of leaving your place assigned in the heavens.

Autumn will grow longer.
Your oceans will crash more closely to shore.
You will note more cloudy days, but experience less rain.

When you see these things taking place,
know for certain your star is following its instinct,
searching for secret dimensions draped in the fabric of space.

How large it will seem in your sky;
how brightly it will sparkle!—
and how strongly it will pull you to follow.

Instinct, you know, draws a moth to the flame.
But here there is no flame. Only a black hole.

AN OLD MAN'S FIRST DAY ON PATMOS   *William Foy Coker*

wild waves surge and thunder
salt breeze fills my beard my eyes
ears hair on this treeless headland

gulls glide above hazy tumbled troubled rocks
pierce with cries of joy or woe or insistence
that noise any noise must rise from living throats
lest these desolate crags be wakened

desolate not by my choice but yours
for you always did favor
the desolate lonely barren forlorn
whether choosing people or places

no boats no nets no knowledge of saltwater fish
and no strength left in back arms legs anyway

ah Simon Peter ah James in old days
we could have dived into something new
learned salty ways here
plied our trade in the deep
but we were called to other fisheries
and the emperor's crossed wood overturned
our world the royal sword cut short
everything with you with us

Father Zebedee gone too
your mossy boats baking under Galilean suns
bottoms up beside piles of rotten nets
reeking fish fish fish

Mother Salome you always wanted the best
for your boys the glory the heights
well here I am the highest point for miles—
but you're gone.
Mother Mary of tender heart

conversant with angels
how did you deal with the blessed
unexpected messages they brought?
how remain graceful yielding attentive
glowing till the end?

all these voices silenced this side
of heaven's gates—and who knows
what's on the other?
you promised preparation Jesus
you promised many mansions
but what can this mean?
something beyond my vain
imagining for sure

Holy Spirit opener of ways and minds
lifter of heads hands hearts
even death-bound bodies
giver of peace truth consolation
can this rough dragging be your leading?

Lord you rolled my raging thunder
into love's calm call
needed my heart for your work
kneaded my stony heart
softened it for your work
you haven't spared me here so far
from my beloved little children
for no reason I know

what blessing what task is set before
these brittle bones aching joints stiff fingers?
what sights what visions remain
for these clouding eyes
beneath dark swift heavy ripping clouds
love's banner over my weary head?

SIGNS OF THE TIMES

Nathaniel A. Schmidt

After Nicolas Pousin's Landscape with Saint John on Patmos

Despite this landscape's details, luscious
laurels, earthen ruins, distant city,

my eyes, trained by television,
photographs, and newspaper accounts,

preconditionally consider this image
unrealistic, an Elysium fantasy,

as Saint John reclines on Patmos,
adorned in the Word's gilded robes

while he receives Revelation, not quite
how I compose verse in a suburban study,

but if I'm willing to let this piece
speak, the action itself a grace,

why wouldn't Apocalypse's creation
be pastoral, its stylus tracing our way to truth?

Amidst this Edenic setting,
so romantic I nearly disbelieve,

attentiveness perceives contemporary
temples, ancient only from context,

with their ecclesiastical columns
reminiscent of Philadelphia, Pergamum, Rome,

broken and strewn about the apostle's
feet, resting at the start of a dusty road

that courses through uneven terrain,

gullies, ravines, to a bridge's causeway,

and stuck between conception and death,
an enigmatic land both alive and empty,

I sense an innate desire to cross over,
needing an unnatural structure

to usher me into the city, celestial,
rising up on the horizon, peering through trees –

the aforementioned artists, pundits, and prophets
whose solitary scrolls are recorded

in an obelisk that reaching into the azure,
heaven, anticipating our God's decent.

THE HORSEMEN   D.S. Martin

Inspired by the woodcuts of Albrecht Dürer (1471–1528)

In the depth of a dark dark night   down in the ravine
the wind comes up & stirs the leaves of the myrtle trees
where a corral of shadowy horses grow restless
Your approach is barred by a rider on a red horse   his hand
rests on the hilt of his sheathed sword You ask   *Whose
are these and why are they here?*   His reply   *Come and see*

But that's when a thundering voice shouts   *Come*
& a powerful white stallion pulses from the black woods
Its rider has an arrow notched in his bow   The wreaths blow
back from his hair   & from the garlands in his horse's mane
We are the ones sent to roam the earth   the first rider says
to ride to the four compass points & to hold back the wind

Beware the coming of pestilence   he continues   *Beware
the coming of wild beasts that leave a country childless
the coming of famine   & the one*   he adds as his heel
digs into his horse's flank   *the one who brings a sword*
He too rides off as the voice roars   *Come*   leaving you
alone beneath the breathing myrtles

You walk toward the whinnying herd   & see starlight
shimmering on their coats   brown & black & white
red & dappled   *Come*   the voice echoes through the ravine
& a black horse & rider race past   almost hitting you
with the scales he carries   He shouts   *No bread
no bread   but plenty of distractions for the well fed*

You feel drawn to pick up a three-tined pitchfork   & toss hay
into the corral   The strong horses push against each other
begin to kick & bite   You offer hay to a skeletal pale nag
He doesn't fight   as you impulsively climb onto his back
You lift the trident in your hand   With unexpected strength
he surges to a gallop at the sound of the command   *Come*

About the Poets

Ryan Apple has lived in Michigan his entire life, despite his strong distaste for all things winter. Since 2006, he has been privileged to serve as music professor and financial aid director of his alma matter, Great Lakes Christian College. Ryan is blessed to be part of Delta Community Christian Church along with his wife Darcie and their school age children.

Christine Boldt, a retired librarian has lived in Texas for thirty-five years. She was a Peace Corps Volunteer in Nigeria in the 1960s, and lived in Italy during the 1970s. Christine has published in *Christianity and Crisis, the Washington Post, the Dallas Morning News*, and *Working Mother*. Her poetry has appeared in *Christian Century, Windhover, the Texas Poetry Calendar, Enigmatist, the Poetry Society of Texas Book of the Year*, and *Encore*.

James E. Cherry is the author of three volumes of poetry, a collection of short fiction and two novels. His latest novel, *Edge of the Wind*, was published in 2016 from Stephen F. Austin University Press. He has been nominated for an NAACP Image Award, a Lillian Smith Book Award and a Next Generation Indie Book Award. He has an MFA in creative writing from the University of Texas at El Paso. Cherry resides in Tennessee with his wife where he is preparing another full length collection of poetry. He can be reached on the web at: jamesEcherry.com

William Foy Coker is a native of the Arkansas Ozarks who has lived most of his adult life in Nebraska. His poetry has been published in *Nebraska Life, Windhover, The Cape Rock, Petersburg Press*, and *thebookden.blogspot.com*. A former mathematics teacher, he is also a songwriter with over sixty

About the Poets

titles registered with CCLI. A 30th anniversary issue of his *Kingdom Songs* has just been released.

Todd Davis is the author of five books of poetry, most recently *Winterkill* and *In the Kingdom of the Ditch*, both published by Michigan State University Press. He also edited *Fast Break to Line Break: Poets on the Art of Basketball* and *Making Poems: Forty Poems with Commentary by the Poets*. He is a fellow of the Black Earth Institute and teaches environmental studies and creative writing at Penn State University's Altoona College.

Nellie deVries' poems have appeared in *Peninsula Poets* and *The 55 Project*. Her three children's books were published by Baker Book House. When she isn't working as a nurse, she enjoys reading, hiking and spending time with family in Michigan.

Sandra Duguid's poetry collection, *Pails Scrubbed Silver*, was published by North Star Press (2013). Her poems have appeared in *Meta-Land: Poets of the Palisades II*, *Modern Poetry Studies* and *Anglican Theological Review* among others. She earned degrees from Johns Hopkins (MA), and the University of Buffalo (Ph.D.). The NJ State Council on the Arts awarded her a Fellowship in Poetry. For 25 years, she taught at colleges in the metro New York-New Jersey area, most recently at Caldwell University, and at East Stroudsburg University in Pennsylvania. She and her husband, Henry Gerstman, live in New Jersey.

Judith Deem Dupree's new book, *Sky Mesa Journal*, is published by Wipf and Stock. She was a founding member, Board member and teacher in the San Diego Christian Writers Guild. Judith initiated and directed Ad Lib, a yearly creative arts workshop/retreat (1996-2010). A Board member of *Ruminate* Magazine, she blogs frequently on their web site. Her personal blog is www.judithdeemdupree.com. Her pending work is in theater drama.

Diane Glancy is professor emerita at Macalester College. Her 2014-15 books: *Fort Marion Prisoners and the Trauma of Native Education* (nonfiction), *Report to the Department of the Interior* (poetry), *Uprising of Goats, One of Us* and *Ironic Witness* (novels), Wipf and Stock. A new collection of poetry, The *Collector of Bodies: Concern for Syria and the Middle East*, was published by Wipf and Stock, in 2016. Other books are listed on her websites: www.dianeglancy.com, www.dianeglancy.org

Ona Gritz's poetry collection, *Geode*, was a finalist for the 2013 *Main Street Rag Poetry Book Award*. Her poems have appeared in *Ploughshares*, *Bellevue Literary Review*, *Beauty is a Verb: The New Poetry of Disability* and elsewhere. Ona's chapbook of poems, *Left Standing*, was published by Finishing Line Press in 2005. Her novella-length memoir, *On the Whole: a story of mothering and disability* is available from Shebooks.

David Brendan Hopes is a poet, playwright, and painter who lives in Asheville, North Carolina. He has appeared in such spiritual anthologies as *The Sacred Place*, *Odd Angles of Heaven*, *Upholding Mystery*, and *The Best American Spiritual Writng, 2008*

Rod Jellema, emeritus Professor of English, University of Maryland, directed the creative writing there for 20 years. He began writing poems in mid-career (1967) and has published seven books of them. The recipient of two poetry writing fellowships from the National Endowment for the Arts and several awards for his poems and translations, he is currently at work on a book called, *Finding the Undercurrent: Short Essays on the Reading, Writing, and Teaching of Poetry*.

Laurie Klein is the author of *Where the Sky Opens* (Cascade Books) and *Bodies of Water, Bodies of Flesh* (Owl Creek chapbook winner). A past recipient of the Thomas Merton Prize, her work has appeared or is forthcoming in *The Anglican Theological Review*, *Christian Century*, *Plough Quarterly*, *Barrow Street*, *The Southern Review*, *Tweetspeak*, and the new bestselling anthology, *River of Sky: Poems for the Twenty-first Century*.

Philip C. Kolin is the University Distinguished Professor in the College of Arts and Letters at the University of Southern Mississippi (Emeritus) where he also edits the *Southern Quarterly*. He has published over 40 books, including eight collections of poems, most recently *Departures: Poems* (Negative Capability Press, 2014); *Emmett Till in Different States: Poems* (Third World Press, 2015); and *Benedict's Daughter: A Collection of Poems* (Wipf and Stock, 2017). Kolin has also published a widely used business writing

About the Poets

textbook, *Successful Writing at Work*, now in its 11th edition with Cengage Learning.

Cameron Alexander Lawrence is a graduate of the University of Arizona and lives in Decatur, GA, where he shares a home with his wife and three young daughters. His poems have appeared or are forthcoming in *West Branch, Image, Pittsburgh Poetry Review, Asheville Poetry Review, the Orison Anthology*, and elsewhere.

Christina Lee holds an MFA from Seattle Pacific. Her writing can be found in *The Toast, Hoot, Relief, Ruminate*, and *Whale Road Review*. She lives with her husband in Sierra Madre, CA, where she teaches English at a public junior high. She's an avid-yet-tragically-slow trail runner and a bumbling pianist. Her books are organized by color.

John B. Lee, Poet Laureate of the city of Brantford in perpetuity and Poet Laureate of Norfolk County for life, is the author of over seventy published books. His work has appeared internationally in 500 publications and he is the recipient of 100 international awards for his writing. He lives in a lake house overlooking Long Point Bay in Port Dover, Ontario where he works as a full-time author.

Mary Lee lives in Galway, Ireland. She has a background in Psychotherapy and Spirituality. Her poems have appeared in *Skylight 47; Orbis; The Linnet's Wings; The Galway Literary Review; Time of Singing* (award winner); *Crannog; The Furrow; Spirituality; The Poet's Quest for God*, (2016, Eyewear Publications, UK); and *The Passion Poetry Magazine* (competition award winner). She is a contributor to *A Living Word*, RTE Radio 1. Her debut poetry collection, *Bloom* appeared before Christmas, 2016 (Matthew James Publishing Ltd.).

Kathryn Locey chairs the Humanities Department at Brenau University in Gainesville, Georgia, where she also teaches literature and writing. Her poems have appeared in various publications, including *Natural Bridge, Able Muse, Paper Nautilus*, and *The Christian Science Monitor*.

Marjorie Maddox: Sage Graduate Fellow of Cornell (MFA) and Professor of English at Lock Haven University, she has published eleven collections

About the Poets

of poetry—*including True, False, None of the Above; Local News from Someplace Else; Wives' Tales; Transplant, Transport, Transubstantiation*; and *Weeknights at the Cathedral* —the short story collection *What She Was Saying* (Fomite), four children's books; *Common Wealth: Contemporary Poets on Pennsylvania* (co-editor); and 500 stories, essays, and poems in journals and anthologies. Please see www.marjoriemaddox.com

Matt Malyon is a jail/juvenile detention chaplain with Tierra Nueva, and a Reader in the Orthodox Church. He holds an MFA from the University of British Columbia. His poetry has appeared in various journals—including the University of Iowa's *100 Words, Rock & Sling, Christianity & Literature*— and has received a Pushcart Prize nomination. He is the founding director of Underground Writing, a literature-based creative writing program serving at-risk communities.

D.S. Martin is the author of three poetry collections, most-recently *Conspiracy of Light: Poems Inspired by the Legacy of C.S. Lewis* (Cascade). He is the Series Editor for the Poiema Poetry Series from Cascade Books, and has recently edited both this anthology, and *The Turning Aside: The Kingdom Poets Book of Contemporary Christian Poetry*.

Julie L. Moore is the author of three books of poetry: *Particular Scandals, Slipping Out of Bloom*, and *Election Day*. Her poetry has appeared or is forthcoming in many anthologies and journals, including *Alaska Quarterly Review, The Christian Century, Image, Nimrod, Poetry Daily, Prairie Schooner, The Southern Review*, and *Verse Daily*. You can learn more about her work at julielmoore.com.

Annabelle Moseley is an award-winning poet and writer, born and raised on the North Shore of Long Island, where she resides with her husband and children. Author of nine books, Walt Whitman Birthplace Writer-in-Residence (2009-2010) and Long Island Poet of the Year (2014), Moseley is founder and editor of *String Poet*, the online journal of poetry and music. She is a Lecturer of Religious Studies and Literature at St. Joseph's Seminary and St. Joseph's College in New York.

R. William Muir's lyrical poetry has been set to music in a variety of forms: from hymns, anthems and a cantata, to a blues opera that updates the Book

About the Poets

of Job, setting the action in a blues bar and transforming Job into a "latter day Eric Clapton." For the past 30 years, the wordsmith has earned a living as a reporter, photojournalist, editor and proofreader, currently with *Canadian Mennonite* magazine.

Violet Nesdoly lives near Vancouver B.C. and has had poetry published in *Prairie Messenger, Utmost ChristianWriters.com, Time of Singing, Your Daily Poem,* and others. Her work has been included in several anthologies, she has published two books of poems, *Calendar* (2004) and *Family Reunion* (2007), and the novel *Destiny's Hands* (2012). She loves trying out new poetic forms and writes often about nature and faith. Find out more about her and her work at VioletNesdoly.com.

Christine Valters Paintner is an American poet and writer living in Galway, Ireland and the author of ten books of nonfiction on creative process and contemplative practice including *The Artist's Rule*. She is the founder of AbbeyoftheArts.com, a virtual monastery dedicated to monastic spirituality and the arts. Her poems have been published in *The Galway Review, Headstuff, Skylight 47, Presence,* and *Spiritus Journal*.

Barbara Colebrook Peace is the author of two poetry books, *Kyrie* and *Duet for Wings and Earth*, both published by Sono Nis. She also co-edited *P.K. Page: Essays on Her Works* (Guernica). She has read her poetry on CBC, taken part in literary festivals and concerts, and contributed to various journals and anthologies. She lives in Victoria, B.C., Canada.

Eric Potter is a professor of English at Grove City College (PA) where he teaches courses in modern poetry, American literature, and creative writing. His poetry has appeared in many publications, as well as in the anthology *Imago Dei: Poems from* Christianity and Literature. He is the author of two poetry chapbooks, *Heart Murmur* and *Still Life*, and a full-length collection, *Things Not Seen* (Wipf and Stock).

Debbie Sawczak has been writing poetry since high school. Her poems have appeared in such publications as *Crux, Writual,* and the *U.C. Review*, but have enjoyed exposure mainly through countless public readings, including the Eden Mills Writers' Festival, community events, coffee houses, and church liturgies. Debbie particularly admires Eliot, Hopkins, Donne,

About the Poets

and Kenyon. A member of the Ecclestone writing group (Brampton, Ontario), she is married and has three adult sons.

Angeline Schellenberg's first book, *Tell Them It Was Mozart* – linked poems about raising children on the autism spectrum – was published by Brick Books in fall 2016. Her poetry has appeared in numerous journals and was shortlisted for *Arc* Poetry Magazine's 2015 Poem of the Year. A Mennonite publication copy editor, she holds an MA in Biblical Studies. Angeline lives in Winnipeg, Canada, with her husband, two teenagers, and a German shepherd/corgi.

Nathaniel A. Schmidt holds a Bachelor's degree in English literature from Calvin College, and a Master's degree, also in English, from the University of Illinois, Springfield. He has taught for Spring Arbor University, Jackson College, and Grace College. His first poetry collection, *An Evensong*, is published by Resource Publications, an imprint of Wipf and Stock. Originally from the Chicago-land area, he currently resides in southwest Michigan.

Jean Bouwman Schreur has been writing ever since high school, when her English Literature teacher wrote encouraging words to her on a writing assignment. She has written worship material for her church and also for a small church publication. She belongs to a writing group that meets monthly. Jean is a retired nurse and lives on the family celery farm in Michigan with her husband, Richard. They have a son, Craig, living in Seattle, WA.

Luci Shaw was born in London, England in 1928. A poet and essayist, since 1986 she has been Writer in Residence at Regent College, Vancouver. Author of over thirty-five books of poetry and creative non-fiction, her writing has appeared in numerous literary and religious journals. In 2013 she received the 10th annual Denise Levertov Award for Creative Writing from Seattle Pacific University. *The Thumbprint in the Clay*, essays on beauty and purpose in the universe, was released in 2016, as was *Sea Glass: New & Selected poems*. She lives in Bellingham, WA.

Marjorie Stelmach's fifth volume of poems, *Falter*, has recently appeared in the Poiema Poetry Series from Cascade Books. Previous volumes include: *Without Angels* (Mayapple), *A History of Disappearance*, and *Bent upon Light* (Tampa). Recent work has appeared in *Boulevard, Cincinnati*

About the Poets

Review, Florida Review, Image, New Letters, and *Prairie Schooner* among others.

Margo Swiss has three books of poetry, most recently *The Hatching of the Heart* (Wipf and Stock). She has edited an anthology of Canadian poets, *Poetry as Liturgy* (St Thomas Poetry Series) and two books on Milton and other Renaissance writers: *Heirs of Fame* (Bucknell UP) and *Speaking Grief in English Literary Culture: Shakespeare to Milton* (Duquesne UP). She teaches at York University, Toronto.

John Terpstra has published nine books of poetry and four non-fiction. His work has won the CBC Radio Literary Competition Prize for Poetry and several Hamilton Literary Awards, and been shortlisted for the RBC Taylor Prize and Governor General's Award for Poetry. One of his poems, "Giants", is mounted on a Bookmarks Project plaque at the edge of the Niagara Escarpment overlooking downtown Hamilton, where he lives and works as a cabinetmaker and carpenter.

Ben Volman is a freelance writer based in Toronto and the author of *More Than Miracles: Elaine Zeidman Markovic and the Story of The Scott Mission* (Castle Quay Books, 2015). His poetry has appeared in the *University of Toronto Review.*

Paul Willis is a professor of English at Westmont College and a former poet laureate of Santa Barbara, California. He recently served as an artist-in-residence in North Cascades National Park. His latest collection is *Getting to Gardisky Lake* (Stephen F. Austin State University Press, 2016). pauljwillis.com

Acknowledgements

Christine Boldt: "Dumbstruck" first appeared in 2015, in *Windhover, A Journal of Christian Literature*, published by the University of Mary Hardin-Baylor Press.

Todd Davis: "Jonah Begins to Think Like a Prophet," "Nicodemus's Complaint," and "Ananias Lays Hands on Saul." From *The Least of These*. East Lansing: Michigan State University Press, 2010. Copyright © 2016 by Todd Davis. Reprinted by permission of the author.

Sandra Duguid: "The Forerunner" first appeared in *Anglican Theological Review* and "Memorials" first appeared in *Christianity and Literature*. Both poems are from *Pails Scrubbed Silver*. Thanks to the editors at North Star Press, St. Cloud, MN.

Ona Gritz: "Rebecca Pregnant" first appeared in *Nine Mile Magazine*. "Abraham's Hand" first appeared in *The Pedestal Magazine* and was republished in *Your Daily Poem*.

Rod Jellema: "Words Take Water's Way." from *Incarnality: the Collected Poems of Rod Jellema* (Eerdmans, 2010). Copyright © 2010 Rod Jellema.

Philip C. Kolin: "Hagar's Lament" originally appeared in *Penwood Review* 7 (2003): 12; "Magdalen" in Philip Kolin's *A Parable of Women*. Itta Bena, MS: Yazoo River Press, 2009; and "St. Peter on the Eternity of Three" in Philip Kolin's *Benedict's Daughter: A Collection of Poems*. Wipf and Stock, 2017.

John B. Lee: "Visiting the House of Bread" and "Via Dolorosa" are from the poetry collection *Let Us Be Silent Here*, Sanbun Publishing, 2012.

ACKNOWLEDGEMENTS

Kathryn Locey: A version of "Shiphrah and Puah: Midwives in Egypt" appeared in Kathryn Locey's doctoral dissertation, *In Eyes Not His: New Glimpses of Biblical Women*.

Marjorie Maddox: "Esau's Lament", "Lot's Daughters", and "The Prophesy of Birds" first appeared in *Christian Century*. "Joseph of Arimathea" first appeared in *Christianity and Literature* and is from *Weeknights at the Cathedral* (WordTech). "Lot's Daughters" is from *What She Was Saying* (Fomite Press). "The Fourth Man" first appeared in *Dappled Things* and is from *True, False, None of the Above* (Poiema Poetry Series). "God Tries on Skin" is from *Weeknights at the Cathedral* (WordTech), and has appeared in *A Widening Light: Poems of the Incarnation* (Harold Shaw Publishers), and *How to Fit God into a Poem* (Painted Bride). "In the Basket" first appeared in *Vineyards*. "Jacob Wrestles with God" is also from *True, False, None of the Above* (Poiema Poetry Series).

D.S. Martin: "Nothing For It" first appeared in *In Touch*, "James The Less" in *Anglican Theological Review*, "Thomas Didymus" in *Christian Century*, and "The Horsemen" is from his collection *Poiema*, Wipf & Stock, 2008.

Julie L. Moore: "Enoch", "Elisha's Bones", and "Lines" are from *Slipping Out of Bloom*, published in 2010 by WordTech Editions, Cincinnati, Ohio. "Confession" and "Wonder" are from *Particular Scandals* (Wipf and Stock Publishers).

Annabelle Moseley: The following poems were previously published in *A Ship to Hold the World and The Marionette's Ascent: A Double Volume of Poetry by Annabelle Moseley* (2014, Wiseblood Books): "Job Addresses God", "God Answers Job", "The Sacrifice", "Rebekah Speaks of Jacob", "Miriam Witnesses Moses' Adoption".

Violet Nesdoly: "Present" was first published on the blog Violet Nesdoly / Poems in January, 2016 vnesdolypoems.wordpress.com and "Ananias explains the situation to Sapphira" was first published in *Time of Singing*, 2013/14 Winter Issue.

Acknowledgements

Christine Valters Paintner's "There Is No Time for Love to Be Born" originally appeared in her book, *Illuminating the Way: Embracing the Wisdom of Monks and Mystics*, published by Ave Maria Press in Notre Dame, Indiana. Reproduced here by permission.

Barbara Colebrook Peace: "Song of God: for Judas not yet born" originally appeared in the book *Duet for Wings and Earth* by Barbara Colebrook Peace, Sono Nis 2008.

Eric Potter: "Almost Apostle" previously appeared in *Still Life* (Franciscan University).

Angeline Schellenberg: "Faith" appears in Angeline Schellenberg's full-length poetry collection *Tell Them It Was Mozart* (Brick Books), fall 2016. "Storing Up Treasure" first appeared in the *MB Herald*, August 2013.

Luci Shaw is deeply grateful to all the editors and publishers who brought her work into print over the years. This includes WordFarm, Pinyon Press, Wm. B. Eerdmans, Wipf & Stock, Regent College Publishing and Paraclete Press.

Marjorie Stelmach: "The Apple and the Knife" first appeared in *Boulevard* and is included in *Falter* (Poiema Poetry Series, Cascade Books, 2016).

Margo Swiss: "Pentecost" was first published in *Poetry as Liturgy: An Anthology of Canadian Poets,* ed. Margo Swiss (St. Thomas Poetry Series, 2007).

John Terpstra: "Outburst: the Widow of Zarepheth" was previously published in *Two or Three Guitars: Selected Poems* (Gaspereau Press, NS; 2006). Used with permission. "Martha's Trouble" and "The Disciple Cradles in His Arms the Dead Christ" were previously published in *Poetry as Liturgy: An Anthology by Canadian Poets* (ed. Margo Swiss, The St Thomas Poetry Series, Toronto ON, 2007).

Ben Volman: Versions of "Amos Speaks at the Richmond Street Exit" appeared in the online site of The Messianic Literary Corner (www.

Acknowledgements

messianic-literary.com) and in *Shatter the Moon*, Poems by Ben Volman (Chapbook edition: Visible Press, 2000) as "Don Valley & Richmond Heading West."

Paul Willis: "Daniel to the Chief of the Eunuchs" and "A Stone for a Pillow" first appeared in the *Lamp-Post* —"Inviting a Friend to Supper" first appeared in *Christianity and Literature* —"Mysterious Ways" first appeared in *Christian Century* —and "The Thirteenth Apostle" first appeared in *Perspectives*.

The Poiema Poetry Series

COLLECTIONS IN THIS SERIES INCLUDE:

Six Sundays toward a Seventh by Sydney Lea
Epitaphs for the Journey by Paul Mariani
Within This Tree of Bones by Robert Siegel
Particular Scandals by Julie L. Moore
Gold by Barbara Crooker
A Word In My Mouth by Robert Cording
Say This Prayer into the Past by Paul Willis
Scape by Luci Shaw
Conspiracy of Light by D. S. Martin
Second Sky by Tania Runyan
Remembering Jesus by John Leax
What Cannot Be Fixed by Jill Pelaez Baumgaertner and Martin E. Marty
Still Working It Out by Brad Davis
The Hatching of the Heart by Margo Swiss
Collage of Seoul by Jae Newman
Twisted Shapes of Light by William Jolliff
Where the Sky Opens by Laurie Klein
These Intricacies by David Harrity
True, False, None of the Above by Marjorie Maddox
Falter by Marjorie Stelmach
Phases by Mischa Willett
The Turning Aside by D. S. Martin
Second Bloom by Anya Krugovoy Silver
Your Twenty-First Century Prayer Life by Nathaniel Lee Hansen (forthcoming)

www.ingramcontent.com/pod-product-compliance
Lightning Source LLC
Chambersburg PA
CBHW030114170426
43198CB00009B/623